God the Artist

God the Artist

Revealing God's Creative Side Through Pottery

Morgan McCarver

NASHVILLE

NEW YORK • LONDON • MELBOURNE • VANCOUVER

God the Artist

Revealing God's Creative Side Through Pottery

Published in New York, New York, by Morgan James Publishing. Morgan James is a trademark of Morgan James, LLC. www.MorganJamesPublishing.com

Proudly distributed by Publishers Group West®

Scripture taken from the *ESV® Study Bible (The Holy Bible, English Standard Version®)*, Copyright © 2008 by Crossway, a publishing ministry of Good News Publishers. Used by permission. All rights reserved.

Morgan James BOGO™

A **FREE** ebook edition is available for you or a friend with the purchase of this print book.

CLEARLY SIGN YOUR NAME ABOVE

Instructions to claim your free ebook edition:
1. Visit MorganJamesBOGO.com
2. Sign your name CLEARLY in the space above
3. Complete the form and submit a photo of this entire page
4. You or your friend can download the ebook to your preferred device

ISBN 9781636982038 paperback
ISBN 9781636982045 ebook
Library of Congress Control Number: 2023936317

Cover & Interior Design by:
Christopher Kirk
www.GFSstudio.com

Cover Concept by:
Morgan McCarver

Flower designs drawn by:
Morgan McCarver

Photos taken by:
Morgan McCarver

Morgan James PUBLISHING Builds with... **Habitat for Humanity®** Peninsula and Greater Williamsburg

Morgan James is a proud partner of Habitat for Humanity Peninsula and Greater Williamsburg. Partners in building since 2006.

Get involved today! Visit: www.morgan-james-publishing.com/giving-back

*This book is solely dedicated to my Lord and Savior,
Jesus Christ, who is the only reason it exists.
Thank You for every experience, good and bad, that allowed
me to have material for writing this book. Thank You for
guiding me on my own creative journeys and for allowing me
to honor You by writing about some of them here.
Please let me reflect Your glory and allow readers to see Your
beauty and creativity as the Ultimate Artist You are.*

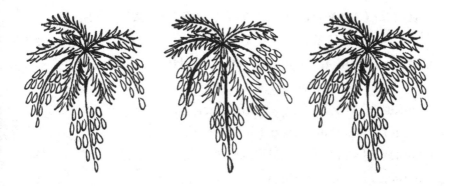

Table of Contents

PART 2: CLAY REFLECTS GOD'S RELATIONSHIP

Introduction

I t is wonderful that you are here! I am honored to welcome you. So many things had to align for this exact moment, and by the grace of God, they have! This project has taken years to culminate in the finished product, but God put the to write a book on my heart even years before.

I remember loving reading and writing growing up. As I got older, I was more drawn to (and still am) reading nonfiction. It was amazing to me that someone else's ordinary life could be worthy of recording and reading. I remember keeping a diary as a young girl, and those entries are quite boring and uneventful, but I still had a desire for record-keeping and a hope that my story would one day be important enough to share. God didn't give me the desire to seriously consider writing this book until I graduated college, but He has been preparing me for writing my story for years.

I know this book was in His plan for my life before I was ever born. He is that powerful! After it became apparent that the three years of wearing my scoliosis corrective back brace were not enough to straighten my spine, I remember begging God to spare me from the corrective surgery. I distinctly remember His response. This is the first time I remember a clear response from God. He told me that my story would not be complete without the surgery. Even though that was a physically and mentally challenging time that required me to work through healing for years, I now agree with God. My surgery recovery time gave me my first experience in a pottery studio. Without my surgery, my love for ceramics might have never been discovered, meaning this book would not exist. I am the person I am today because of that surgery. The circumstance that I thought at the time was the worst possible thing in my life is the catalyst that "springboarded" my entire life. God led me through every step, and through the surgery, I grew closer to Him.

I felt God calling me to record the rough skeleton of the book when I graduated with a ceramics degree. Through several passages in the Bible, I began to recognize pottery symbolism and decided that I should record it so I wouldn't forget. I then tried to find a book to read that would simply compare the Bible verses about clay with actual examples in pottery. Not finding a book I wanted to read propelled me into writing one.

As I began writing down the pottery symbolism, I quickly realized, having not read the Bible all the way through, that there could be clay references I was missing out on and didn't even know it. This is the point where I decided to buy a copy of the Bible that would engage me in reading, the ESV Archeology Study Bible, and began reading cover to cover. My only reading plan was to finish the entire Bible, side notes and all.

Ever the impatient one, I finished the manuscript before I finished the Bible, or at least I thought I did. I was rejected by multiple publishers but was told I could pay a good bit of money to self-publish if I wanted, but I'd also need hefty editing. At this point, I asked God, and I know that He told me I needed to wait and revisit this idea when I had more experience. I honestly thought that meant a couple of decades. Turns out it was three years. In that span of time, I had a job working the sales and support side of ceramics, taught ceramics classes in the evenings, experienced a global pandemic, moved to another state to become a pottery apprentice for over a year, and launched my own business and studio practice. I also finished reading the Bible all the way through. It took me three years to read at my own pace, but by the grace of God, I finished.

As soon as I finished reading, God gave me three more goals: to find a place to serve in my new home church, to actually publish the book, and to go to the Holy Land. I began serving as a youth leader to a precious group of young ladies. I then began editing the manuscript I had begun 4 years prior and realized it needed to be rewritten. During cold January days in the mountains in Asheville, North Carolina, I rewrote the entire book in about two weeks. At that point, I began looking once again for a publisher. Terry Whalin with Morgan James Publishing has been absolutely amazing throughout the entire process. He told me first that I'd need to about double my word count for a book like this to even be considered. A week and a half later, I submitted that lengthened manuscript and gave it all to God.

This has been the first experience in my life where I completely gave the whole process to God. Of course, there have been days of worry and stress, but God is the one who initiated this desire, so I knew it would only happen if it was in His will. Praise God it was! Getting the publisher's acceptance letter was surreal, and every experience since then has been truly fascinating. Now, I guess I'll have to work on getting to the Holy Land!

I hope this book makes you think. Of course, I hope to teach the non-potters about ceramics and the non-Christians about the love of Jesus, but what I want for you to get most importantly from this book is that the God-given gift of creativity is within every one of us to use for our joy and for His glory. I hope you get messy. I hope you acquire a horde of new art supplies. I hope you shine your light and begin recording your own story in your own way. Let this be a guide to help you to grow spiritually and creatively, but please remember I am only human. I make mistakes. The true path can be found by following Jesus and reading His word. My mere musings are not a rule book, simply a prompt. Let the creativity challenges at the end of each chapter be the creative boost you have been looking for. I pray that your relationship with God will grow and change as you see Him in a new light within these pages.

Blessings,

Morgan

PART 1

Recognizing Creativity

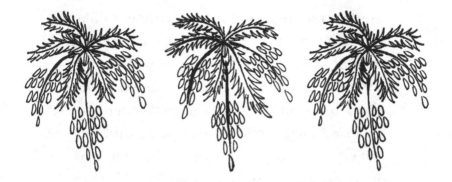

Chapter 1:

Every Human Being Is Creative

"The LORD said to Moses, 'See, I have called by name Bezalel the son of Uri, son of Hur, of the tribe of Judah, and I have filled him with the Spirit of God, with ability and intelligence, with knowledge and all craftsmanship, to devise artistic designs, to work in gold, silver, and bronze, in cutting stones for setting, and in carving wood, to work in every craft'" (Exodus 31:1-5).

"And he has inspired him to teach, both him and Oholiab the son of Ahismach of the tribe of Dan. He has filled them with skill to do every sort of work done by an engraver or by a designer or by an embroiderer in blue and purple and scarlet yarns and fine twined linen, or by a weaver—by any sort of workman or skilled designer" (Exodus 35:34-35).

"And Moses called Bezalel and Oholiab and every craftsman in whose mind the LORD has put skill, everyone whose heart stirred him up to come and do the work. And they received from Moses all the contribution that the people of Israel had brought for doing the work on the sanctuary. They still kept bringing him freewill offerings every morning" (Exodus 36:2-3).

Have you ever been so excited to work on a new creative project that it completely consumes your thoughts until you give yourself the time to work on it? You're going about your daily life—getting groceries, doing laundry, going to work—but in the midst of all that, you are mulling over this grand project, which you are just bursting at the seams to start.

I'll be driving down the road, but my mind is calculating what supplies I'll need and how much time each step in the creative process will take. That's probably not the safest example I could have given you, but hey, I'm a little art obsessed. Some of my earliest memories are learning to sew with my grandmothers and making little farm animals out of homemade dough. At this point, you might have guessed (and you'd be right) that thankfully, my family supported and encouraged my creative interests.

I believe every human being has the capacity to be creative. I can make this statement because the Bible tells me this is true. It tells us multiple times in multiple ways throughout the Old and New Testaments that human beings *are* creative.

That's the reason, in *God the Artist,* we will study verses throughout Scripture that will point back to the creativity God granted us.

One amazing story that doesn't get a lot of pulpit time is the story of Bezalel. God specifically gives Bezalel the ability to create beautiful things for His temple and tells Moses of these talents, that He has given Bezalel the ability "to work in every craft" (Exodus 31:1–5). I would love that God-given ability! God informs Moses that He has given Bezalel this power to make all the things that will be used by Aaron for his priestly duties. God gives creative ability to be used to glorify Himself.

When it is time for Moses to lead the people to construct the Tabernacle, Bezalel is ready and waiting. What's even more beautiful is that Bezalel didn't keep his God-given talent to himself. He didn't demand all the glory and recognition. Moses tells the people that God has put the desire to teach into Bezalel, and he says that Bezalel isn't alone. God also has called "Oholiab the son of Ahismach of the tribe of Dan" (Exodus 35:34b). Together, these two will teach the rest of the Israelites to build the Tabernacle.

In the next chapter, we see Bezalel and Oholiab leading the other skilled workers. We know they are talented craftspeople because the Bible tells us that these were "craftsman in whose mind the LORD had put skill, everyone whose heart stirred him up to come and to do the work" (Exodus 36:2). Not only did God give them the divine talents to perform the skills needed for building the Tabernacle, but He also stirred their hearts with a desire to do the work! God provides everything we need. In this crazy world, it is nice to know that God has a plan and He is willing to share it with us!

Think back to your answer to the first question I asked you. *Have you ever been so excited to work on a new creative project that it completely consumes your thoughts until you give yourself the free time to work on it?* What if that desire is coming from God? What if the thing you think is just a fun side project is actually something God has given you the desire for and is asking you to honor Him through?

If God was calling me to help design and construct the Tabernacle, I wouldn't just give Him my scrounged up spare minutes at the end of each day. I would wake up early, excited to work on what He called me to do because there is so much joy found in living out one's purpose. I would take my time with each detail because I would want it to be good enough for Him. The finished result would be something I am proud of.

Now, don't panic. This book is not recommending that you quit your day job and become a full-time builder of tabernacles. My goal is to reveal all the beautifully hidden symbols of God's love through creativity and art-making. I want you to truly see just how special the creativity God gave you really is. Stop taking your creativity for granted or, even worse, forgetting it altogether. You are a child of God! He has given you not only the *right* to be creative but also the *capacity* for genuine creativity!

I want to guide you on this creative journey to see how our creativity is spiritually rooted in God. It is a God-given skill that we all can use to praise and glorify Him. The purpose of this book is to show the creativity of God and reveal that He has instilled that same imagination inside you too. We have the freedom to create in a world that God created because He loves us enough to give us the free will (imagination) to create.

You might be shaking your head as you read this, saying, "I'm not very good at the *artsy* stuff. If you could see my Pinterest fails that are now adding to the landfill, you'd see that I'm not creative." Loved one, hear me when I say this truthfully: the fact that you attempted a creative project proves that you are creative! I don't claim that we are all art *geniuses*, and I agree that some of us are more talented in different areas than others, but we have all been made creative! God designed each one of us to be creative.

There's a reason you chose to pick up and read this book, which is a good indicator that you may know in what ways you are creative.

Creativity can come in many forms. Of course, painting and drawing, good solid art forms, are probably the first things that come to mind. Creativity is actually a very broad and all-encompassing term, but to fully understand the definition of creativity, we must first look at its root word. The Merriam-Webster definition of the word *create* is "to bring into existence; to produce or bring about by a course of action or behavior; to produce through imaginative skill; design; and to make or bring into existence something new."

Yes, creativity most definitely means art forms like dance, music, theater, and writing. It also includes the visual arts, like painting, drawing, photography, pottery, sewing, and needlework. This standard technical definition focuses on bringing things into existence that didn't yet exist in the world. This might be thinking up new ideas, making new designs, cooking a meal you whipped up from scratch, devising a strategy, braiding your hair differently, redecorating your living area, training a dog, color-coding a calendar, trying a new workout, or making a new lesson plan. Each is just as creative as the last. Some of the more uniquely obscure ways of being creative include board game design, topiary pruning, writing elevator music, designing fabric prints, greeting card writing, and the list goes on. Of course, there are many more ways of being creative, but if I listed them all, that would be a whole other book.

Think about the areas in your life where you are creative. These are most likely things that you enjoy doing. Do you enjoy baking bread? Color-coding your laundry? Hosting a podcast? Singing in the shower? Rearranging the furniture? Upcycling clothing? Pressing flowers? Or choreographing a Zumba routine?

How do you use your creativity for yourself, and how might you use it to glorify God? Children are perfect for this example.

Give a toddler finger paint, chalk, or a box of crayons. What do you think will happen? Try to put yourself in that situation mentally as a child. Most likely the little one will joyfully create with the tools given. The feel of the paint is different and exciting. Moving your entire body, you can fully express your energy with the chalk. You can run, holding the fat stick to the ground, watching a line form behind you. The crayon's waxy substance will be left behind on the paper if you push hard enough. Take all the paper off the colorful stick of wax and now you can roll the entire crayon across the page with one hand! Are you remembering the childlike joys of creating?

When the toddler is finished with her masterpiece, what does she do? Staying in this mindset, what would *you* do? Most likely, the first thing would be to run and show whoever is near you. You'd want to show off the finished product that brought you so much joy in the experience. If it is something transportable, you would probably give it as a gift to your parent or guardian. Do you remember making cards for your family? You wanted them to know that you thought they were special enough to have a piece of your art. Of course, you wanted the praise too; we all like to hear encouragement and reassurance, but that's not why we made the thing in the first place. No, we wanted to feel the joy and excitement of creating.

Now think about a time when someone else's creativity blessed you. Have you ever seen a live play and been so enthralled in the story that you forgot the characters are actors? Has a mural on a wall downtown made you stop and smile? Has a song moved you to tears? Did a child give you one of her drawings? Does walking through an art museum make you feel calm and empowered at the same time? Have you made audible *yum* noises while eating a cupcake? Did a funny story make you involuntarily start smiling? The beauty in receiving someone else's creativity is that beauty and art aren't transferred like money. If someone makes you a cake, they have found joy in the baking, but their joy is not lost once you receive their gift. Surprisingly, it is amplified! They come to us smiling, cake in hand. We can almost feel their joy, which makes us joyful. Then we are smiling! When we see the cake, we get even more excited, which makes them happy at our excitement with their creation, and the joy and positivity expand. When we give a gift, especially something we have made, we are blessing others, which makes us feel unintentionally good! This blesses the Father.

One time, when I was in middle school, I received a card from an anonymous student a few years younger than me. She had handwritten me a note just telling me that she looked up to me and hoped I was doing well. She had drawn some flowers at the bottom of the page. I don't think the note was more than a couple of sentences long. On the surface, it was only notebook paper and words written with a blue ballpoint pen, but it was one of the most thoughtful gifts I had ever received. It wasn't because it was masterfully created or poetically written. Honestly, if anyone else saw it, they probably wouldn't find it that special. But to me, it was extraordinary. To this day, I have no idea who the mystery note was from, but it brightened my day then and still does now. I have kept it after all these years as a sweet reminder of what an ounce of kindness can do. Her note didn't say anything profound. It truly was the thought that counted. She cared enough to give me a note, and that still means the world to me. I know God gave her the creativity, inspiration, and courage to write and send it.

We all have the ability and desire to be creative. I know you might doubt that, but hear me out. Every human being on the planet Earth is in some way creative. How do I know? How can I make such a blanket statement about the entire world? I know every one of us is creative because God created us in His image! If we believe the Bible is true, then we must take *all of it* as truth, and in doing that, we must believe that God created each of us with the capacity for creativity. Why would He do this? Because every creative aspect reveals more of Him and points us back to Himself.

At the end of each chapter, you will be given a creativity challenge. These are purposefully designed to be vague. Creativity should not be forced. It flows out of you naturally in a beautiful way, honoring God. Each challenge can be completed in a variety of ways, so feel free to try a new artistic technique, or play it safe with the stuff you know. But this would be a great time to find your creative ability by trying a new creative outlet each week. If you already have a passion, hone your craft by focusing your skill on that one medium. Please feel free to go as outside the box as you want with these challenges! If you feel comfortable, I would love to see your results! Send me pictures or videos!

Creativity Challenge: We are all creative in unique and different ways. Be a blessing to someone today with your creation!

(Since this is your first one, I'll give you some examples: make muffins and share them with a neighbor or coworker, call a sick or downcast friend and sing them a song, tell a joke to your grocery store cashier, make a card and send it to a veteran or someone living in a nursing home, paint a rock and leave it for someone else to find, help a friend organize her closet, sew warm clothing for those in need . . .)

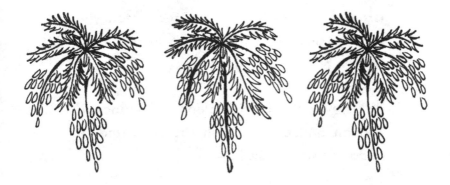

Chapter 2:

We Are Creative Because We Are Made in God's Image, and God Is Creative

"In the beginning, God created the heavens and the earth. The earth was without form and void, and darkness was over the face of the deep. And the Spirit of God was hovering over the face of the waters" (Genesis 1:1-2).

"But now thus says the LORD, he who created you, O Jacob, he who formed you O

Israel: Fear not, for I have redeemed you; I have called you by name, you are mine" (Isaiah 43:1).

"Whatever the LORD pleases, he does, in heaven and on earth, in the seas and all deeps" (Psalm 135:6).

"Then God said, 'Let us make man in our image, after our likeness. And let them have dominion over the fish of the sea and over the birds of the heavens and over the livestock and over all the earth and over every creeping thing that creeps on the earth'" (Genesis 1:26).

"So God created man in his own image, In the image of God he created him; Male and female he created them" (Genesis 1:27).

"Then the LORD God formed the man of dust from the ground and breathed into his nostrils the breath of life, and the man became a living creature" (Genesis 2:7).

"The grass withers, the flower fades, but the word of our God will stand forever" (Isaiah 40:8).

"And why are you anxious about clothing? Consider the lilies of the field, how they grow: they neither toil nor spin, yet I tell you, even Solomon in all his glory was not arrayed like one of these. But if God so clothes the grass of the field, which today is alive and tomorrow is thrown into the oven, will he not much more clothe you, O you of little faith?" (Matthew 6:28-30).

"And God saw everything that he had made, and behold, it was very good. And there was evening and there was morning, the sixth day" (Genesis 1:31).

"Now out of the ground the LORD God had formed every beast of the field and every bird of the heavens and brought them to the man to see what he would call them. And whatever the man called every living creature, that was its name" (Genesis 2:19).

We can't get too far into reading the Bible until we run face-first into the creativity of God. The author of Genesis wastes no time in telling us about it. In the first sentence of the first chapter of the first book in the Bible, we have it: "In the beginning, God created the heavens and the earth" (Genesis 1:1). The first verb in the entire Bible is *created*! We can't move any further into the scriptures until we acknowledge that God is a creative God, and He loves His creation.

I encourage you to go back and read the creation story. It is a beautiful reminder of just how imaginative God is and how little we are compared to His glory. It is also important to note that as soon as the earth was created, even though it was still formless and dark, "the Spirit of God was hovering over the face of the waters" (Genesis 1:2). God's presence is always with His creation! How comforting is that? Just like when we make something we are proud of and say a part of us is represented in our creation, so does God!

I have a really cool Bible that I think is worth giving a shout-out to here. As soon as I graduated from college, I realized—like so many of us do—that I was now living in what the adults call "the real world." That summer after graduation, I realized time was long overdue for me to take my faith into my own hands. I chose and bought myself a Bible that I would get the most out of and be encouraged to read. Praise God, there are so many translations! (Please consider researching and choosing the right one for you.)

After some deliberation, I went with the ESV Archeological Study Bible because I love the cultural references and mini-history lessons included in the margins. I want to understand why passages are written the way they are, and I want to know what the first audience would have been thinking and feeling at the time. It has proven to be an incredible study aid, and I recommend it to anyone who wants to get a better grasp on the history surrounding the text, which brings me to a great example here in Genesis 1.

In Genesis 1, verse 3, God begins to name His creations. He gives names to day and night. The notes in my Bible elaborate on the phrase "God called" in reference to Him naming day and night. It reads, "In antiquity, when a king named an object he was reflecting ownership or dominion over it." God was not just telling us what His creations were to be called, like a painter putting that fancy title plaque below the frame. God was telling everyone that He made these things, and He alone was in control over them. He owned them as His creation.

We, too, as human beings, have been named by God. He tells us in Isaiah, "Fear not, for I have redeemed you; I have called you by name, you are mine" (Isaiah 43:1b). So God created us and named us. That means that we are His creation, and He has authority over us. The psalmist reminds us, "Whatever the LORD pleases, he does, in heaven and on earth, in the seas and all deeps" (Psalm 135:6). God has authority over us regarding governments, bosses, spouses, and even ourselves.

I'm beginning to feel like I'm writing one of those geometry proofs where everything relies on something else, and by explaining the situation through spiraling logic, we finally end at a conclusion that we somehow figured was true all along. God is creative. We are God's creation. We know we were created by God because the Bible tells us He made us and called us by name. He called us by name, displaying His authority over us, and He made us in His image, therefore making us creative as well. Whew! I feel so much more empowered and energized going through all of that. I'm a protected and cherished child of God. I also have all this creative energy that God ordained. God took His time when creating us.

The very last things God chose to make were human beings. We see this in Genesis 1:26–31. God, talking to the Holy Spirit and Jesus (remember they are the Trinity), says, "Let us make man in our image, after our likeness. And let them have dominion over the fish of the sea and over the birds of the heavens and over the livestock and over all the earth and over every creeping thing that creeps on the earth" (Genesis 1:26). In a way, God created us as abstract self-portraits. He created human beings to have similarities to Himself, but we are not gods. Human beings are designed to reflect God's attributes.

In Genesis 2, we get more detail. We learn, "The LORD God formed the man of dust from the ground and breathed into his nostrils the breath of life, and the man became a living creature" (Genesis 2:7). God created His first human being—Adam—from clay! We are made from the earth and connected to it. I am a potter, so clay is kind of a big deal to me. Sure, ceramics look all glamorous on social media, but you've got nothing if you're not willing to get your hands dirty.

This comes into play in Genesis 2:7. God made Adam out of the dust from the ground. God was willing to come down to earth and get covered in mud, specifically to make human beings. We aren't told how God made the birds, plants, water, animals, or even the heavens. God wanted us to know that He is willing to come to meet us where we are, stuck in the mud, and create a new life for us. He shows us this in the New Testament when Jesus is born in a box full of animal feed. We are God's special creation. No other living thing is created in God's image, and yet He still has authority over it all.

God graciously gives humans ownership over the animals. We see in Genesis 2:19 that Adam is naming the birds and animals. Just as God showed authority over day and night by naming them, He is allowing Adam to have dominion over the creatures of the earth by naming them. God then makes woman—Eve—out of one of Adam's rib bones. So yes, ladies, we too are derived from clay.

God chose to share creativity with us. He could have withheld His imagination; I mean, the earth is so intricately and naturally beautiful. Just count how many types of flowers come to mind! And that is only flowers! They won't even last a year; "The grass withers, the flower fades, but the word of our God will stand forever" (Isaiah 40:8). God intentionally made flowers to be fleetingly beautiful to show us His majesty.

Even the flowers teach us a lesson about creativity. Jesus reminds us to "consider the lilies of the field, how they grow: they neither toil nor spin, yet I tell you, even Solomon in all his glory was not arrayed like one of these. But if God so clothes the grass of the field, which today is alive and tomorrow is thrown into the oven, will he not much more clothe you, O you of little faith?" (Matthew 6:28–30). God shows us His love for us through the flowers. If He can give so much time, imagination, and attention to a little flower, how much more must He care for us?

After each of His creations, the author tells us, "God saw that it was good" (Genesis 1:10b). God is perfect, and everything He does and chooses to make will be perfect for His plan as well. He was pleased with His creation. We, however, live in a fallen world. We are not perfect; God did not choose to give us that characteristic of His because, instead, He gave us a choice—and imagination. He allows us to make independent decisions, and sometimes, we make them poorly. Sadly, the first things Adam and Eve physically created were clothes to cover the shame of their nakedness and disobedience to God. Genesis 2:7 tells us, "They sewed fig leaves together and made themselves loincloths" (Genesis 2:7). Ok . . . but I do have to say kudos to them for sewing wearable clothing for their first art projects ever! Too bad it wasn't under different circumstances.

All kidding aside, though, have you ever made something that seemed like a great idea in your head, but the final result fell short in every way? This usually happens to me in the kitchen. I recognize that things would probably go better if I just follow a recipe instead of substituting ingredients for things I like better and simply "winging it" in the end. Family and friends have very graciously swallowed some of my creative flops. I have learned that not everyone truly appreciates nutmeg like I do. I have also made dinner recipes that sound good, but in the end, even *I* can't get them down. We live in a fallen world. We make mistakes. Recipes are misleading. Winging it can be dangerous if you don't know how to fly. Whatever the reason, some things just don't turn out for us because we simply aren't God.

Many creative types have had the same feelings of not measuring up to even their own standards. We can see that perfect vision, but we can't recreate it. One of my favorite books, *Art and Fear: Observations on the Perils (and Rewards) of ART-MAKING*, by David Bayles and Ted Orland, says it best:

Fears arise when you look back, and they arise when you look ahead. If you're prone to disaster fantasies, you may even find yourself caught in the middle, staring at your half-finished canvas and fearing both that you lack the ability to finish it, and that no one will understand it if you do.

More often, though, fears rise in those entirely appropriate (and frequently recurring) moments when vision races ahead of execution. Consider the story of the young student—well, David Bayles, to be exact—who began piano studies with a Master. After a few months' practice, David lamented to his teacher, "But I can hear the music so much better in my head than I can get out of my fingers."

To which the Master replied, "What makes you think that ever changes?"

That's why they're called Masters. When he raised David's discovery from an expression of self-doubt to a simple observation of reality, uncertainty became an asset. Lesson for the day: vision is always ahead of execution—and it should be. Vision, Uncertainty, and Knowledge of Materials are inevitabilities that all artists must acknowledge and learn from: Vision is always ahead of execution, knowledge of materials is your contact with reality, and uncertainty is a virtue.

Imagination is in control when you begin making an object. The artwork's potential is never higher than in that magic moment when the first brushstroke is applied, the first chord struck. But as the piece grows, technique and craft take over, and imagination becomes a less useful tool. A piece grows by becoming more specific . . . Finally, at some point or another, the piece could not be other than it is, and it is done (p 14–16).

We all are the same in this phenomenon. We envision the final product in our heads so much more clearly than once we begin creating. Why does this happen to everyone? Our visions are not fully realized. We are more focused on the emotions and themes surrounding that idea in our heads than on what the finished product might actually look like. For most of us, even if we deeply consider what we are imagining up there in our brains, the final result is still fuzzy. We can't get a clear picture because the art does not exist yet, which is the whole point of creating—bringing something new into existence that has not existed before.

These authors go on to explain that the uncertainty we face when it comes to making art turns out to be a great asset. Of course, we will always have a vision before we begin. Why else would we begin? The feelings of uncertainty and risk are what make the experience of creating truly worth it. You have decided to invent. You become both vulnerable and strong. You reveal your weaknesses throughout your process, exposing them to the real world. It can be terrifying but freeing as well. Fears about art-making aren't as scary once we look them dead in the eyes and decide to move forward regardless of the outcome. Plus, we can always try it again if it fails.

Don't ever be afraid to try, and remember, the piece in progress is not the final result. Every attempt that didn't meet your specifications is proof of a learning experience. Try, make notes, adjust and correct, try again, make more notes, tweak a step, try another time, and the cycle continues. Art-making is cyclical. It has to be. Sure, you start a project, and then in a matter of weeks, months, or years, you bring it to completion, but hasn't that just opened your mind to a dozen more possibilities you are willing to try? Like the toddler with her finger paints, doesn't the joy of the experience make you want to relive it again and again?

Most well-known artists and creatives aren't famous for their first tries at a masterpiece. They have hundreds of practice runs, some sub-par work, and then some pieces they continued to create after the masterpiece. Creativity doesn't stop when we get that one project right; it is ingrained in our lives—and becomes inescapable. Speaking of which, I think I'll have another go at that recipe.

 *Creativity Challenge:* Read and reflect on Genesis 1. Be inspired by the poetic language and the limitless creativity of the God we serve. He has given you the creative energy needed to finish that project you've had rolling around in your head. Give that dream another go this week!

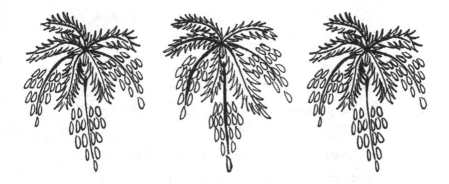

Chapter 3:

We Are God's Creation, Therefore We Are Creative

"The thief comes only to steal and kill and destroy. I came that they may have life and have it abundantly" (John 10:10).

"Let everything that has breath praise the LORD! Praise the LORD!" (Psalm 150:6).

"For we are his workmanship, created in Christ Jesus for good works, which God prepared beforehand, that we should walk in them" (Ephesians 2:10).

"He answered, 'I tell you, if these were silent, the very stones would cry out.'" (Luke 19:40).

"Whatever you do, work heartily, as for the Lord and not for men, knowing that from the Lord you will receive the inheritance as your reward. You are serving the Lord Christ" (Colossians 3:23-24).

Why is it so important to be creative? Why did I write this book on creativity?

Being creative reflects God's nature. Simply, it honors our Heavenly Father. From our earliest ages, we are encouraged to be creative. We are taught silly songs and how to dance. "The Itsy Bitsy Spider" is one of the first songs we ever learn how to sing, complete with hand motions too. Why? Sure, its underlying theme is about perseverance, but a two-year-old won't pick up on that automatically. What they first experience is the creativity and fun. We are given a box of crayons or maybe some watercolor paints. Our parents might stick us in a ballet class. We build forts in our living rooms out of pillows and sheets. I doubt you can go a day in kindergarten without being creative. It's ingrained in our nature!

Creativity allows us to express ourselves in ways that others might understand, including communicating things we might *not* be able to share verbally. Think of cave paintings and hieroglyphics. Pictures are some of our earliest forms of communication and record-keeping. And airplane safety cards include pictures today. They are essential for communicating with those who do not share the same language.

Our creative results also help us better understand ourselves as we get older. Our artistic endeavors teach us who we are.

While we are learning letters and numbers, we are also being taught colors and shapes. Why is it that artistic ability lies on an equal playing field academically in preschool, but by the time we graduate from high school, most of us only take that one required art class "for the credit?" Where did we lose our artistic expression? Somewhere between elementary school choir and the SAT exam, we are taught that creativity and art aren't nearly as important as "knowledge," but the crazy thing is that creativity requires knowledge too (color theory, music theory, line memorizing techniques, budgeting, etc.). I'm not saying there's anything wrong with studying math, history, and science. I loved school and still love learning. My top spiritual gift is knowledge. I'm asking you to consider artistic ability as having equal academic validity to chemistry, geometry, or language arts. I mean, there's even an English class called Creative Writing! Art becomes a hobby, music is pushed to the extra-curricular activities, and dance is categorized as a cardio event. Creativity has been watered down to follow-the-leader-style wine-and-painting classes and quick crafts to support our mental health. Why do we turn to crafts for mental health? Because we don't get enough of it in our daily lives! We physically and mentally need to be creative. That is how God made us.

We are unknowingly stunting the growth of our God-given artistic abilities. By the time we have assimilated into the work-force, we are no longer looking to creatively express ourselves on a daily basis. Right about now, you're probably saying, "What was all of that then in Chapter One? I thought we were all creative without really even knowing it?" And you'd be right. I stand by that statement. I believe that we can't help but create. But this world has been tainted by sin, and the world will happily feed us the lie that creativity is a waste of time.

Look at all the creativity that came from quarantining during the COVID-19 pandemic. When people were at their lowest, they turned to creative outlets. They still do. Crazy, right? We were confined to our homes, unable to experience human contact or public activity. We were afraid for our safety and the lives of those we love. We were stressed and exhausted. We didn't know whom to believe, what to agree with, or whom to trust. What did we turn to? Art—the thing that schools are pulling funding from, the one general education course we had to take to graduate, the home economics class that doesn't even exist anymore. These were the activities that kept people sane during one of the greatest global hardships we've faced in our lifetime. I mean, grocery stores ran out of yeast because so many people wanted to bake bread from scratch! That's right, yeast!

Many people founded small businesses out of that terrible environment. It almost became a renaissance or rebirth of craft, but then how many of us just "normalized" after it was over? How many of us returned to our over-packed schedules that repel creativity? We used art

"We use art as a crutch instead of as a vitamin."

as a crutch instead of as a vitamin. We should take a dose of creativity every day! If it makes us more joyful in the experience, then why are we choosing to be joyless?

It is in our nature to create, but we don't always recognize and praise God for our creativity. We can't help but be creative, and yet we struggle to take the time to intentionally use our skills. We choose not to find beauty and meaning in this world because it takes up too much of our time. We let social media hand us a fill-in-the-blank template for beauty. "Use this filter and this audio with your pictures." Is this what creativity has been reduced to? Sadly, I believe yes.

It is God's nature to create beautifully, and He gave that likeness to us as well. Just as the "thief comes only to steal and kill and destroy," the devil is trying to steal your artistic expression right out from under you (John 10:10a). He doesn't want you to find joy in creating. He hates beauty because it points us back to the beauty of God. Jesus ends John 10:10 by saying, "I came that they may have life and have it abundantly" (John 10:10b). Satan wants you drained, bored, and distracted.

Using your imagination allows you freedom from this world and gives you the ability to enjoy a glimpse of Heaven. Following the monotonous head-down drone of the crowd keeps you in line with the world's values—just get ahead and make more money. Like the true Master of His craft, God wants us to look in awe at the creativity surrounding us; He desires us to express ourselves artistically through the means He's provided. Jesus came to give us all life: a purpose on earth, a future in heaven, and an abundant experience through Him. He allows us to relish in our and others' creative talents because He gave them to us to make our lives more abundant!

We can be inspired by others' creativity as well. Think of the people singing from their balconies during the pandemic. Remember the individuals willing to make video tutorials leading you through the creative process? Even if they are not Christians, they unknowingly have the ability to praise God. Here is an excerpt from a great resource, Got Questions, which elaborates on a Jewish belief:

It has been said that the Jewish sages associated the covenant name of God, Yahweh, with breath. The idea is that the name itself, when pronounced, is the sound of breathing: the two syllables of the name correspond to the intake and outtake of a single breath. In this way, the theory goes, our breaths evoke the name of God. A naturally voiced inhalation sounds like "Yah," and a voiced exhalation sounds like "Weh." Thus, with every breath we take, we are speaking God's name. He breathed into us the breath of life (Genesis 2:7), and we still retain that breath . . .

When the natural act of breathing is viewed in this light, the name of God is everywhere. Atheists and agnostics acknowledge Him constantly. A baby's first cry is a calling out to God. The sighs of a sufferer are wordless appeals to the God who hears. And when we cease speaking God's name, we die.

This is such a powerful thought for me to hold on to while I go about my daily life. God signed His creation by allowing us to say His name with every breath. Psalm 150:6 says, "Let everything that has breath praise the LORD! Praise the LORD!" By this theory, we can't help but praise Him. I think this concept is pretty amazing. Every breath taken on earth is a signature of the Creator. We involuntarily and audibly represent the Artist who made us. God's artistic signature is visibly hidden inside every breathing thing on earth.

Breathing as Glory

Within the past few years, I have taken an interest in breathing techniques. There are many theories and ways of going about it, but my goal was to find a way to capture and tame my anxious thoughts. Deep breathing in a specific pattern has helped me to stop the unwanted and destructive thoughts that seem to over-power my mind and instead replace them with the peace of God through repeating Bible verses to the flow of my breath. I learned of this Jewish belief after I had taken an interest in breathwork, but the "coincidence" seems surreal. Yes, deep breathing allows more oxygen to my brain and requires me to slow down and focus, but I also choose to match my breathing to the cadence of certain Bible verses, depending on my situation. I was calling out to God through repeating the verses, but unknowingly, I was calling out to Him just by breathing!

This Jewish belief is not taken directly from Scripture. You won't find any verses about this in the Bible. We most certainly can be breathing and, unfortunately, dishonor God. This theory is just something worth considering. For me, it is interesting to think about God giving us the ability to glorify Him with every breath.

Talents as Glory

I think one of the "forgotten" ways of glorifying God is through creativity and talents. Speaking of talents, are you familiar with Jesus's parable of the talents? In this context, a talent was a form of payment, like a coin. My ESV Archeological Study Bible tells me that in the New Testament, one talent was equal to "6,000 days (just over nineteen years of work)" for a common laborer. You'll find the full parable described in Matthew 25:14–30.

In the parable of the talents, Jesus compares God to a master, and we are His servants. The master gives various amounts of talents to three servants, "to each according to his ability" (Matthew 25:15). Two of the servants use the resources wisely. They did business with what their master had given them, and when the master returned, were able to double their talents and return them to the master. The third hid his talent in the ground and only returned to his master what he had given him in the first place. The master is very pleased with the first two servants, but he gets rid of the last servant altogether, calling him lazy. This parable shows us that we, as Christians, should use the resources God gives us to further His Kingdom. He gave us these gifts on earth so that we could bless others and spread the Gospel in our own, effective ways.

Think for a second: what if we allowed talents to symbolize our actual talents instead of money? God not only gives us physical resources but also spiritual gifts and talents—areas in our lives where we are naturally strong. Reread this Bible passage and think about what talents you have. Apply them to this parable.

If God has given you a gift for singing, but you never sing to glorify God, then when you get to Heaven, you are only returning the talent God gave you. You have not grown it through practice and training. You have not been able to bless others and invest in them through the talent God gave you because you buried it within yourself instead of using it to show God through your life.

If we are to truly believe that God has given us our creativity and our talents, then we must not hesitate to use them for His glory. In Exodus 15, Moses leads the people in song after having just crossed the Red Sea. In verse 20, Aaron's sister Miriam leads the women in singing, dancing, and playing the tambourine. They use their talents to lead the people in corporate praise and worship of the God who just led them out of Egypt.

David wrote much of the poetic book of Psalms. These verses are beautifully soaked in imagery and are where a lot of us turn when in need of biblical sustenance. Because David followed through and wrote down (or dictated) his songs and poems to God, he unknowingly blessed us years—generations—into the future. Where would we be without Psalm 23?

"The LORD is my shepherd; I shall not want. He makes me lie down in green pastures. He leads me beside still waters. He restores my soul. He leads me in paths of righteousness for his name's sake.

"Even though I walk through the valley of the shadow of death, I will fear no evil, for you are with me; your rod and staff, they comfort me.

"You prepare a table before me in the presence of my enemies; you anoint my head with oil; my cup overflows. Surely goodness and mercy shall follow me all the days of my life, and I shall dwell in the house of the LORD forever" (Psalm 23).

Most Christians know it by heart. David honored God through his talents.

We have to remember that we are God's "workmanship, created in Christ Jesus for good works, which God prepared beforehand, that we should walk in them" (Ephesians 2:10). God designed each of us to have different creative talents to fill different daily needs. He places us on paths where we can use our skills to honor Him; to choose not to is a waste of our talents. Jesus tells us that even if we are silent in our praising God, "The very stones would cry out" (Luke 19:40). God's creation will honor Him, no matter what, and I want to make sure I'm included in His creation! How embarrassing it would be to get to Heaven and hear God say the rocks had to praise Him because we chose to hide the gifts He gave us.

If we knowingly choose to hide our God-given talents, then we are not fully honoring God. We deny a part of ourselves that He gave us and that He also shares with us. We will be missing out—not only on the joy that comes with using our gifts but also on blessing others and bringing them one step closer to God's Kingdom through our talents.

Remember, God doesn't demand perfection. That is His job. All He asks of us is that we "work heartily, as for the Lord and not for men, knowing that from the Lord you will receive the inheritance as your reward. You are serving the Lord Christ" (Colossians 3:23–24). We don't need earthly recognition or praise because God's provision of our salvation is more than enough. We are free to take risks and try new things because God's grace will cover our mistakes. There is no failure if what we are trying to do is honor God.

 *Creativity Challenge:* Praise God for all of the talents with which He has equipped you. Think back to your childhood. What creative outlet did you love? How did it make you feel to share your joy of creativity with those around you? What creativity did you uncover in the midst of the pandemic? Do you still have your sourdough starter? Is there a half-finished macrame wall hanging lying around? What happened to your book of poetry? Focus on the one talent you think is your strongest. Find a way to give glory, honor, and praise to God by using that talent—today.

On the pottery wheel, the potter is in control of the clay. The clay must be soft and malleable enough to respond to what the potter is asking of it. The potter's hands gently and sensitively guide the clay into the form it is supposed to be, responding to the clay's needs for water or rest.

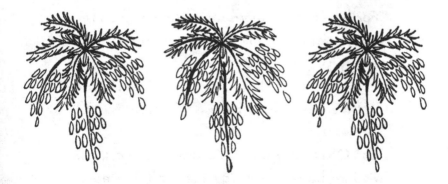

Chapter 4:

All of God's Creation Points Back to Him. How Do I Know? Pottery

"It is he who made the earth by his power, who established the world by his wisdom, and by his understanding stretched out the heavens. When he utters his voice, there is a tumult of waters in the heavens, and he makes the mist rise from the ends of the earth" (Jeremiah 10:12-13).

"For his invisible attributes, namely, his eternal power and divine nature, have been clearly perceived, ever since the creation of the world, in the things that have been made. So they are without excuse" (Romans 1:20).

"O LORD, how manifold are your works! In wisdom have you made them all; the earth is full of your creatures" (Psalm 104:24).

"My frame was not hidden from you, when I was being made in secret, intricately woven in the depths of the earth" (Psalm 139:15).

"Remember that you have made me like clay; and will you return me to the dust?" (Job 10:9).

"What has been is what will be, and what has been done is what will be done, and there is nothing new under the sun" (Ecclesiastes 1:9).

"For from him and through him and to him are all things. To him be glory forever. Amen" (Romans 11:36).

Have you ever tried to pick out a color to paint a room in your house? Or have you tried to match a color? It seems nearly impossible. There are more options than you even knew existed. You thought the paint swatches would narrow it down, but all it did was expand your options to choices you didn't even know you had. How much more expansive are God's imagination and His creation?

God reigns over it all because He made it all. Jeremiah even reminds us, "It is he who made the earth by his power, who established the world by his wisdom, and by his understanding stretched out the heavens" (Jeremiah 10:12). God created everything because of His ultimate power, wisdom, and understanding. God made it all because He is strong enough. He understands everything because of His infinite wisdom. Nothing else deserves our praise.

Throughout the Bible, we can find praise for God's creation. Paul writes to the Romans, reminding them of God's "eternal power and divine nature," saying they have been evident in God "ever since the creation of the world" (Romans 1:20). Ever since living things have existed, they have acknowledged God's might because He created them.

Again in Psalms, David praises God, saying, "O LORD, how manifold are your works! In wisdom have you made them all; the earth is full of your creatures" (Psalm 104:24). The earth is so full of God's creation that we haven't even seen it all in person. Some animals, especially the dinosaurs, were extinct before we even entered the scene . . . maybe that's a good thing for us. I mean—wow! God created some animals knowing full well we would only glimpse their existence by digging up their bones!

Do you have a favorite animal? Maybe it is a pet or even a team mascot. It could even be Leviathan. Maybe you've loved this animal since childhood. I think my favorite animal is the polar bear. The ocean conservancy does a great job providing fast facts. Polar bears are smart and patient when it comes to waiting for food. Their skin is black to absorb heat and their fur is translucent so it won't block the sun. Polar bears go sledding for fun and can swim really fast.

This is all interesting to know, but how does it relate to God and clay and creation? Well, there is no other bear exactly like the polar bear in the entire world. God made bears so different within their own species that there are no two alike. To get even more detailed, no two polar bears are identical. We could do this with every animal and plant on Earth. God's imagination is even more infinite than the paint swatches.

God's power over His creation is such a comforting thought. He gives us, as His creation, power as well. I could not be a ceramic artist if it was not for God's divine guidance. They say to write what you know, and thanks to the grace of God, I know pottery. It is so symbolic of God's relationship with us. I look forward to unpacking that with you through the rest of the book.

I have had an interesting relationship with ceramics. I am probably the last person you would pick to be a ceramic artist. I am allergic to mold, which doesn't bode well for working with wet mud. I am a self-proclaimed germaphobe; yeah, did I mention the moldy mud thing? I am physically not built for strength, and most boxes of clay weigh fifty pounds. Don't even get me started about the strength needed for plaster molds and the pottery wheel. I'm not a big fan of using the pottery wheel, which is basically the most glamorous part of ceramics. Also, I am not physically limber.

I had surgery for scoliosis at Shriners Hospital when I was fourteen years old; two titanium rods and eighteen screws prevent me from moving my spine out of its rigid prison. Like I said, I'm the last person qualified for ceramics, but I know God has given me the talent and drive for it. How do I know? Well, for starters, every time I tried to get another job out of college, I ended up back in ceramics. Second, I wouldn't have found ceramics if it wasn't for my scoliosis.

The summer after my surgery, I was not allowed to dance for a year, which crushed me. My mom signed me and my friend up for a summer pottery camp, and, as they say, the rest is history. I didn't fall in love with clay until that summer camp. The instructor had to carry my clay for me. I loved the feel of the clay and the ability to create virtually whatever I wanted. It was like starting with a blank canvas, but there wasn't even a canvas. I felt completely liberated and unrestricted even through my regimented healing process. Clay provided the malleability my body no longer had. I couldn't get enough of it and ended up taking adult classes after school even though I wasn't an adult yet—just to have access to the studio.

My high school didn't offer any classes, so I went to a local community arts center for my weekly lessons. I loved it. The teachers shaped my relationship with clay, but there was nothing like creating with my hands and learning on my own just what the clay was capable of. One of my teachers became like a grandmother to me, very kind and encouraging. She'd bring in her own materials to let me try different techniques.

My other instructor pretty much left me to my own experiments with very little guidance, but that method also allowed me to grow. Even though he wasn't as hands-on, he let me figure things out independently. He left me to struggle, and I needed that experience to prepare me for what was to come.

I was the youngest in the class by about thirty years. Everyone seemed to take me under their wings. I learned just as many life lessons as I did pottery skills during those nightly classes. It's crazy to think back on it now and realize that I'd stick with pottery after seeing what a hard time I had with the wheel.

I have some incredibly wonky wheel-thrown pieces from those years, but I have kept them because they remind me of how I pushed through and accepted my struggles. I embraced the fact that I was learning, and I salvaged every piece I made. Each misshapen bowl was beautiful to me because I made it. I had complete freedom over the design, even if I couldn't control the clay like I wanted to yet.

I realize now that this is how God sees us. He loves us simply because He *made* us. If anyone else had made those wobbly pieces, I would not have given them a second glance, but those were *my* pieces. I worked on them for days. I spent hours carefully handling them and putting effort into crafting them. I glazed each one and lovingly admired it as if it was the finest work. I still love those pieces dearly because I spent time with them. They hold memories, and they show me where I came from. Praise God that He is perfect and is able to make each of us perfect in His sight for His will. My pottery was unintentionally flawed because I wasn't skilled enough yet to master the craft. God doesn't do anything unintentionally. He is perfect, so He literally can't fail. He is the Master of His craft. Even though we may think we are flawed, God has made us each exactly how He designed us.

The passage I am learning this year is Psalm 139. Verse 15 says, "My frame was not hidden from you, when I was being made in secret, intricately woven in the depths of the earth" (Psalm 139:15). This verse has been hard for me to swallow. Even now, more than ten years after my surgery, I still struggle with body image. I look at my stiff torso and wish things were different. I must tell myself, though, that there is a reason God walked me through that adventure. I honestly believe the main reason was to write this today.

I believe my humble beginnings in pottery were God-ordained, and I believe He has kept me right where I am supposed to be, according to His will. The Lord makes no mistakes in His creations. Probably my favorite passage in the whole Bible is the end of Job. Poor Job has been complaining and going back and forth with his friends about his circumstances for thirty-seven chapters. He even uses a piece of pottery to scrape his sores (Job 2:8). He asks God to "Remember that you have made me like clay; and will you return me to the dust?" (Job 10:9). Job is asking God if he is going to die soon.

Elihu, the smartest and youngest of Job's friends, chimes in with a pottery reference: "Behold, I am toward God as you are; I too was pinched off from a piece of clay" (Job 33:6). He is reminding Job that while he also doesn't understand God's ways regarding Job, he, too, is only human, made from the same "clay."

All of a sudden, a whirlwind arises and God answers Job from the whirlwind. If you ever want to feel God's power, read Job 38–41. Wow! God shows up and gives Job an answer. God tells Job just some of the things that He is in control of, and all Job can do is humble himself in front of God's majesty. The imagery alone is powerful. Every time I read this passage of God's true majesty, I feel safe. I know that may seem like an odd reaction. Yes, I'm in awe of His utter brilliance, but I also am glad that He is my God and He protects His children. Here's some of Job 38:

> "Have you commanded the morning since your days began, and caused the dawn to know its place, that it might take hold of the skirts of the earth, and the wicked be shaken out of it? It is changed like clay under the seal, and its features stand out like a garment. From the wicked their light is withheld, and their uplifted arm is broken. Have you entered into the springs of the sea, or walked in the recesses of the deep? Have the gates of death been revealed to you, or have you seen the gates of deep darkness? Have you comprehended the expanse of the earth? Declare, if you know all this" (Job 38:12-18).

Any one of these things would be impossible for Job, and yet God does them all. We also get a bonus clay reference! Comparing the morning to fresh clay to seal a document (like a wax stamp), God paints a beautiful picture. He compares the new day to new clay, soft and formable under His touch. The seal refers to stamping official documents, once again alluding to God's authority. God stamps each day with His seal, exercising His authority over His creation.

God doesn't approach Job talking about the internet and airplanes. He doesn't show him how electricity will light homes and X-rays will save lives. God knew those things were to come, but Job would never understand them. He meets Job at his level of understanding. God speaks in a way that is easy for Job to get a clear picture. God is in control of Job's situation because He is in control of Job's known world. God graciously humbles Job and reminds him of who is in control.

In Chapter 41, God is referring to the biblical creature Leviathan. Some people believe this animal was a dinosaur of some kind. God asks,

> "Can you draw out Leviathan with a fish-hook or press down his tongue with a cord? Can you put a rope in his nose or pierce his jaw with a hook? Will he make many pleas to you? Will he speak to you soft words? Will he make a covenant with you to take him for your servant forever? Will you play with him as with a bird, or will you put him on a leash for your girls? Will traders bargain over him? Will they divide him up among the merchants? Can you fill his skin with harpoons or his head with fishing spears? Lay your hands on him; remember the battle—you will not do it again! Behold, the hope of

a man is false; he is laid low even at the sight of him. No one is so fierce that he dares to stir him up. Who then is he who can stand before me? Who has first given to me, that I should repay him? Whatever is under the whole heaven is mine" (Job 41:1-11).

My ESV translation explains that Leviathan refers to "the name of a mythological sea monster in Canaanite mythology." It could also reference a crocodile or a hippopotamus, but whatever it is, it is powerful. God, who is even more powerful, reigns over it.

God not only chose to create such an unwieldy beast, but He is still stronger and more powerful than it could ever be. Who are we as human beings to question God's strength? How can we offer Him our meager creativity when He is all-powerful? How can we even hope to create when "there is nothing new under the sun" (Ecclesiastes 1:9b)? Because God, in His infinite wisdom, allows us to serve Him.

Just as how making something for someone else blesses both the giver and receiver, so does praising God. When we praise God, we recalibrate our minds, like God repositioning Job's posture from entitled to humble. We remember that we are not in control. Our praise of God blesses Him, but it also saves us from becoming self-important. We reposition ourselves out of the center of our own attention and focus more on God and His will. We assume the correct posture of bowing to Him, "for from him and through him and to him are all things" (Romans 11:36a). We owe Him everything, so how can we not praise Him?

Creativity Challenge: Find something in nature to truly study. It might be a specific landscape, a bird call, a waterfall, a leaf, or an animal. Find out all you can about it. What makes it special compared to others like it? Try to recreate it. Mold it out of clay, paint it, whittle it, or whatever method you choose. How difficult is it for us to replicate God's creation? Even if I could sew my own polar bear, I can't bring it to life, and that is just one out of the billions of things God has made! Praise Him from whom all creativity flows.

PART 2

Clay Reflects God's Relationship

With His Creation

Notice how dark the clay I'm throwing is. This is natural
South Carolina red clay that I processed straight from the ground.
I had to mix, sieve, and drain the clay to make it workable.

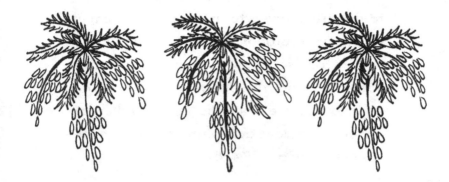

Chapter 5:

The Lifecycle of Clay and How It Relates to Humanity

"By the sweat of your face you shall eat bread, till you return to the ground, for out of it you were taken: for you are dust, and to dust you shall return" (Genesis 3:19).

"For as in one body we have many members, and the members do not all have the same function, so we, though many, are one body in Christ, and individually members of one another. Having gifts that differ according to the grace given to us, let us use them: if prophecy, in proportion to our faith; if service, in our serving; the one who teaches, in his teaching; the one who exhorts, in his exhortation; the one who leads, with zeal; the one who does acts of mercy, with cheerfulness" (Romans 12:4-8).

"Therefore, if anyone is in Christ, he is a new creation. The old has passed away; behold, the new has come" (2 Corinthians 5:17).

D epending on where you are in the world, your soil probably looks different from someone else's. Growing up in South Carolina, I can remember my parents fighting the red dirt, especially in the garden. It was so dense that we would have to wait until after it rained to do any shoveling because the ground would be too dry otherwise. The dirt would hold together so well that I remember making dishes out of it with my backyard playmates. Of course, when the rains came, my little dishes would melt away. I can remember being told not to get in that red clay, which pretty much made up the entirety of the soil in our area. It doesn't come out of clothing! That red stain would seep into the fabric of my clothes and never come out.

What I didn't learn until years later was that red dirt is actually clay that can be harvested, processed, and used. I've fired it a few times. It still stains like crazy, though. Of course, there are easier ways to acquire clay than by processing it yourself.

There are many local ceramics stores throughout the US that make and process clay. There are also international clay companies. I must say, I love a little blue porcelain from Spain! Most of the clay I choose to work with is a white porcelain from Kentucky.

A potter must start with a good foundation. The first step is picking out the clay. Yes, there are air dry clays and polymer clays that are in their own categories, but there are also different types of clays within the world of fired ceramics. Some are better for hand-building, with a grittier consistency that holds up to constant molding and shaping. Others are better for throwing on the wheel, for being more elastic or even smoother on the potter's hands while throwing.

There are also different styles and appearances of clay, depending on the composition of the minerals within it. The chemical makeup of the clay determines whether it looks white like porcelain, red like earthenware terra cotta, black, brown, or speckled, like many stoneware. Each clay has a different feel and must be treated differently. An earthenware clay fires at a lower temperature, allowing for brighter glaze colors since pigment can burn out at higher temperatures. You might be familiar with earthenware terracotta planters, which get their reddish hues from the iron in the clay. Stoneware is more durable to thermal shock, so it is often used for bakeware. Porcelain is translucent and smooth as a result of the finer particles of kaolin and feldspar. It can also be used for bakeware or other things like space shuttle parts and hip replacements (Dr. Steven F. Harwin and Dr. Nolan A. Maher). You might recognize it in your family heirloom china or your bathroom sink.

Bone china is made using bone ash. It is thinner and more translucent than porcelain, making it useful in tea sets. In most basic terms, clay is just purified, formable dirt and water. This clay is what ancient potters choose to work with and what today's ceramic artists choose today. It can be found all over the world.

Does that variety sound familiar? Just like the clay, each of us have different personalities. Have you ever tried to do something that was against your personality type? It's good for us to stretch ourselves, but if you're anything like me, you probably don't love the experience. Praise God that there are different personality types; otherwise, we would all drive each other crazy! The important thing to remember is that we are all human beings; we are all made from the same dust . . . or clay!

Just as human beings have a life cycle, clay has a cyclical life before it gets fired. If the clay gets too wet or too dry, it becomes "reclaim" or recyclable clay. The clay is no longer workable, so it is set aside to mix with other pieces of clay. The artist takes care in blending, blunging, and wedging the reclaim clay into one even, workable consistency to turn it back into usable clay. This process can take days to months. It involves getting the clay to a workable consistency by letting it soak in water, drying it out on a plaster slap, or mixing it with other various wet and dry ingredients. The artist must devote time to prepping clay. Adding water may be necessary to revive an especially dry batch or adding dry ingredients to reconstitute a wet slurry. Sometimes the clay needs to be left in the sun or on a slab of plaster so the water can be slowly absorbed.

Once the mixture has the correct amount of ingredients, the artist will focus on the consistency of the clay. There are de-airing electric pugmills that are great for this step. They'll mix the clay while removing all of the air. Then, you can flip the switch and pipe the clay out of the machine into one long coil, ready for use. Of course, you can still do it the old-fashioned way too. Some artists will put their overly wet clay in pillowcases, tie them closed, and hang them to let the water drain out. You can also set your wet clay onto something that will help absorb the water, like a slab of plaster or a cement board.

When the clay is ready to be worked, it can be wedged. The practice called *wedging* helps move all of the clay particles in one spiraling direction. Clay is wedged by rotating one's hands at a downward angle, similar to kneading dough. The difference is that kneading adds air into the dough, while wedging removes air from the clay. By spiraling the clay, the air bubbles are worked toward the surface and eventually pop out. Wedging also disperses the moisture evenly throughout the clay so there aren't any lumps or surprises when using it. The person wedging the clay must keep both feet firmly planted for a strong foundation with enough leverage to wedge the clay correctly. The arms must apply firm and even pressure to the clay in repetitive sweeping motions. An experienced artist can sense when the clay has been wedged enough. Once the clay flows in a spiraling direction, it is mostly air bubble-free and ready to be used.

The clay must be kept sealed in airtight containers or plastic bags so it won't dry out. If the clay is left uncovered, the moisture will evaporate from it, leaving a hard, unworkable piece of clay. Then you will have to start the mixing process all over again. Clay is so amazing because you can continue to break it down and reuse it time after time. As long as the clay remains unfired, you can reuse it as many times as you want.

Clay starts as dust in the ground and returns to dust if it is never fired. If you make the most glorious clay vase but never actually put it under the heat, it will turn to sludge if it gets wet. In Genesis 3:19b, God reminds us that we are not that different. After Adam and Eve have sinned, God curses the ground and the serpent and unleashes consequences for the first humans. He reminds Adam that he will have to work hard to provide for his family to stay alive "till you return to the ground, for out of it you were taken; for you are dust, and to dust you shall return" (Genesis 3:19b). Our lives are short compared to the grand scheme of things. Like the clay before it is fired, we are fragile. If our body temperature is warmed by two degrees, we have a fever. We are not physically substantial. Our earthly bodies will start to decay before we reach a hundred years of life, but our spirits will live forever.

Since God sent His Son, Jesus, to take all of our sins upon Himself and die in our place, we can have the free gift of eternal life. If we are born-again Christians, our souls will ascend into heaven once our earthly bodies die. If you are not a Christian but would like to be, the choice is before you. The way to eternal life is painless and free for us because Jesus gave everything. All we must do is admit that we are sinners who can't ever hope to erase our mistakes on our own. We must believe that Jesus came to earth, fully God and fully man, and believe He died for our sins and was resurrected after three days. Finally, we must confess our sins to God through prayer and ask Jesus to be the LORD of our lives, in control of our path. Then, we must live our lives in obedience to God's commandments, trusting in Him and seeking His will. If you are missing a personal relationship with God, please contact a Christian or church near you that you trust.

Clay and Humanity

From dust to dust, God has given us such a unique relationship with Him, one that can be better understood through clay. When referring to specific properties of clays, the term used is "clay body!" Even in our vocabulary, we are already connecting clay to humanity. God is the artist who created us. God, "The Artist," made Adam out of the dust, or clay, of the ground. Human beings come from the foundation material of our earth, which comes from the ground; therefore, we are connected to the earth and all things God has made.

He also gives us spiritual gifts. Just as different clay bodies are able to perform better than others in different circumstances, different human beings are better equipped for different tasks. Paul reminds us in Romans that we are all one body under Christ (just as all clay is the same substance), but "the members do not all have that same function" (Romans 12:4). Some Christians work best behind the scenes at building a strong church foundation, while others are gifted at teaching or leading within the church. Just like the clay, we are equipped by God with spiritual strengths that allow us to better serve Him and His church. Paul lists some of these gifts in the New Testament. These skills are talents that are specifically given to Christians by the Holy Spirit to better do the work God asks.

Don't get confused. Spiritual gifts and God-given talents are two different things. They can overlap, but they are not identical. Paul lists out many of the spiritual gifts in Romans. He accounts, "Having gifts that differ according to the grace given to us, let us use them: if prophecy, in proportion to our faith; if service, in our serving; the one who teaches, in his teaching; the one who exhorts, in his exhortation; the one who leads, with zeal; the one who does acts of mercy, with cheerfulness" (Romans 12:6–8). This is not the full list, but these spiritual gifts are attributes that God gives each follower of Christ to better serve the church and others. Looking at the list, there might be one you identify with more than the others. You very well could be stronger in that spiritual gift! Notice how creativity, talent, and artistic ability aren't mentioned. There's another list Paul gives in 1 Corinthians. Let's check it for creativity:

"Now there are varieties of gifts, but the same Spirit; and there are varieties of service, but the same Lord; and there are varieties of activities, but it is the same God who empowers them all in everyone. To each is given the manifestation of the Spirit for the common good. For to one is given through the Spirit the utterance of wisdom, and to another the utterance of knowledge according to the same Spirit, to another faith by the same Spirit, to another fights of healing by the one Spirit, to another the working of miracles, to another prophecy, to another the ability to distinguish between spirits, to another various kinds of tongues, to another the interpretation of tongues. All these are empowered by one and the same Spirit, who apportions to each one individually as he wills" (1 Corinthians 12:4-11).

What a great list of God's power! It is amazing He chooses to bestow upon us strengths in these areas. Again, however, I didn't seem to see anything about creativity. This means that creativity is not a spiritual gift! Why is that so exciting?

Because *everyone* has the capacity for outlandish creativity.

I took a spiritual gifts class about a year ago, and I learned that my top spiritual gifts are related to knowledge, wisdom, administration, and evangelizing. While that might not surprise you since you are reading this book, I was a bit surprised. I never would have said that I was good at administration or evangelism. It did confirm to me my love of knowledge. Through my church, I was able to get connected and serve in a way that expounded on my spiritual gifts. I feel so connected and useful because I was able to find the right fit, and I encourage you to do the same!

If you have never taken a spiritual gifts class or test, I highly recommend it! I think most of us love learning new information about ourselves, and these tests help us not only understand ourselves better but allow us to do God's work more effectively. The interesting thing, however, is that you won't learn about which gift the creative people fall under because creativity is needed in all areas of spiritual gifts. Think back to Part One of this book. If we truly believe that all human beings are creative (and we should because the Bible tells us so), then that means we must also believe everyone is gifted with the talent of creativity. We all have the capability of being creative in addition to our spiritual gifts.

Like the clay that has been recycled and reclaimed, our lives have the capacity for change spiritually. We must remember that "if anyone is in Christ, he is a new creation. The old has passed away; behold, the new has come" (2 Corinthians 5:17). Our unworkable hearts can always be transformed by Jesus. Once we become Christians, our souls are transformed permanently. We have become like the new clay, easily moldable and ready to adjust to God's will.

Consider your spiritual walk right now. Are you feeling open to change for God? Has your heart softened toward His will? Is your life fresh and new for God's use, or are you feeling a little dried out and hard-hearted? If you ask God to reveal to you the areas in your life that you need to work on, then He will. Better yet, you can even ask Him to give you the courage and wisdom to work on those trouble areas in your life, and He will!

 *Creativity Challenge:* Discover your spiritual gift! That might mean taking an online test or getting a book. Take some personality tests and be honest with yourself about your strengths and weaknesses. Then find a way to be creatively connected in your church or community specifically using your strengths and spiritual gifts!

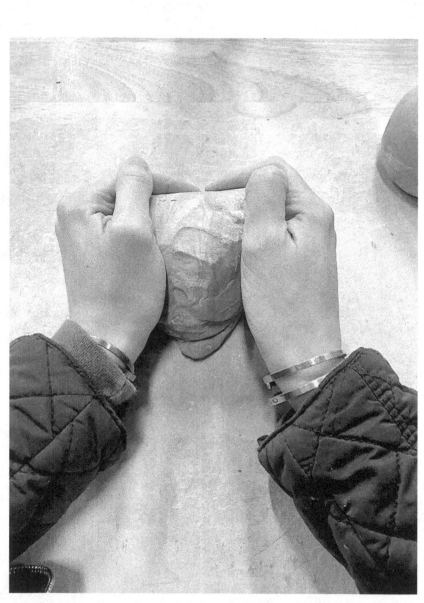

Wedging clay homogenizes the clay particles to give the potter a more uniform piece of clay. It evenly distributes moisture and works out lumps and air bubbles. This process is similar to kneading dough, but instead of working air into the dough, I'm compressing the air out of the clay by working it in a spiral motion.

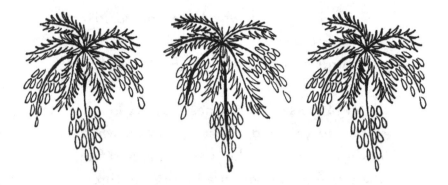

Chapter 6:

Mixing Clay, Quite Literally and Figuratively

"I stirred up one from the north, and he has come, from the rising of the sun, and he shall call upon my name: he shall trample on rulers as on mortar, as the potter treads clay" (Isaiah 41:25).

"And at the ninth hour Jesus cried with a loud voice, 'Eloi, Eloi, lema sabachthani?' which means, 'My God, my God, why have you forsaken me?'" (Mark 15:34).

"My God, my God, why have you forsaken me? Why are you so far from saving me, from the words of my groaning?" (Psalm 22:1).

"John to the seven churches that are in Asia: Grace to you and peace from him who is and who was and who is to come, and from the seven spirits who are before the throne, and from Jesus Christ the faithful witness, the firstborn of the dead, and the ruler of kings on earth" (Revelation 1:4-5).

"The LORD is my rock and my fortress and my deliverer, my God, my rock, in whom I take refuge, my shield, and the horn of my salvation, my stronghold" (Psalm 18:2).

"He has made my flesh and my skin waste away; he has broken my bones" (Lamentations 3:4).

"And as you saw the feet and toes, partly of potter's clay and partly of iron, it shall be a divided kingdom, but some of the firmness of iron shall be in it, just as you saw iron mixed with the soft clay. And as the toes of the feet were partly iron and partly clay, so the kingdom shall be partly strong and partly brittle. As you saw the iron mixed with soft clay, so they will mix with one another in marriage, but they will not hold together, just as iron does not mix with clay. And in the days of those kings the God of heaven will set up a kingdom that shall never be destroyed, nor shall the kingdom be left to another people. It shall break in pieces all these kingdoms and bring them to an end, and it shall stand forever" (Daniel 2:41-44).

Consider the process for making baked goods from scratch. Sometimes the recipe will call for mixing the dry ingredients together and then adding them to the wet ingredients. I know this is especially true with cakes. I'm not really a baker, so I'm sure some of you could tell me a lot better than I'm trying to tell you. I know there's some kind of chemistry that happens when you mix an egg too much, and it gets tough, so instead, you first mix all of the dry ingredients for as long as you want, then you add in your egg and butter, maybe milk and other wet ingredients. You want everything to get as thoroughly mixed as possible for the dough or batter to perform correctly, but you also don't want to over-mix your ingredients or the final product might be too tough or chewy. Making and preparing clay is similar.

If a potter chooses to make her own clay, she will start with dry ingredients. As I mentioned in the last chapter, depending on which clay body she wants to make, she will add different amounts of various raw materials or chemicals. She will then add water to suit how wet she wants the clay. The clay should be wet enough that it holds together appropriately but not too wet that it is more sticky than formable. Of course, today there are electric clay mixers, but in biblical times, the potter would mix by foot!

We get one reference to this in Isaiah 41—a simile comparison at the end of the verse. A person who is coming from the north will "trample on rulers as on mortar, as the potter treads clay" (Isaiah 41:25b). If you don't have an electric mixer in which to mix your clay, then you have to go old-school. Obviously, in Isaiah, they went *very* old-school.

The potter mixes all the dry ingredients together to form a volcano-shaped pile with the dry material on the ground. Picture a mountain of powder, but where the peak would be, the mountain looks more like a donut. The center is caved in, making a ring shape. Water would be poured into this hole, and the powder keeps it from running out of the mixture. The potter then goes barefoot and moves around the mixture in a circular pattern. This little dance will evenly mix the water with the dry ingredients, creating a perfectly blended clay body.

Upon looking at the mixture, you would see you can't separate dry ingredients from each other or from the water. The clay would've been dug wet from a riverbank. Either way, we learn from depictions in Egyptian tombs that the potter's assistants would prep the clay by stomping on it with their feet (Bryant G. Wood PhD). Often the assistants would do the physical labor so the potter could save strength for technique. This also teaches the assistants how to learn the consistency of good clay.

I believe Isaiah 41:25 can be taken literally and figuratively. In Isaiah 41, God begins by comforting His people. He reminds them that He has come to their rescue in the past and that He can be relied on to provide deliverance in the future as well. The end of the chapter shifts, however. God calls out His people for trusting in idols to save them. God says He will send a power from the north to "trample on rulers as on mortar, as the potter treads clay" (Isaiah 41:25b). I believe this is a warning from God to give up idolatry, or foreign kings will overtake you. My trusty Archeology Bible tells me the sun imagery could symbolize Cyrus the Great. God would use foreign nations to attack and punish His people, but He gives them a future hope.

I also believe this verse is foreshadowing Jesus's future coming. The verse mentions calling one up out of the northern region. Mary conceived Jesus from the Holy Spirit in Nazareth, a town to the north of Bethlehem and Jerusalem. Jesus could very well be the one coming from the north. The verse also mentions that this chosen one of God will call upon God's name. Who does that sound like? I started getting chills when God revealed this to me. Jesus calls upon God's name multiple times throughout the New Testament. He shows human beings how to pray, and He also calls upon God as He is dying on the cross. Jesus's last words before succumbing to his crucifixion were, ""Eloi, Eloi, lema sabachthani?" which means, "My God, my God, why have you forsaken me?" (Mark 15:34). He is calling upon God's name, just like the prophecy in Isaiah 41:25 mentions. It also takes us back to the book of Psalms. In Psalm 22, the first line is "My God, my God, why have you forsaken me? Why are you so far from saving me, from the words of my groaning?" (Psalm 22:1). Jesus has referenced this verse word for word.

This imagery of the potter trampling the clay is so much clearer now, knowing exactly how a potter would trample clay.

Not only will God's people be crushed, but they will be scattered, spread apart. They will become mixed in—assimilated into—the culture that overtakes them. They won't just break into two halves like a ceramic jar; they will be broken down into their raw form. This is not necessarily a comforting picture, which is why I believe God intended this verse also to bring hope of a Redeemer who would do the same to the enemy nations of God.

Another reference to Jesus in Isaiah 41:25 points to a leader rising from the sun. Jesus, the Son of God, was resurrected from the dead the morning of the third day after his crucifixion. God is light; we get that from Genesis and the beginnings of the earth. God is more brilliant than the sun. Jesus was sent to be "the ruler of kings on earth" (Revelation 1:5). This would explain the reference in Isaiah 41:25 of the one crushing the rulers on earth. Jesus is the ruler of all peoples and nations; therefore, he conquers all other rulers on earth.

The Goodness of Being Trampled

We all feel trampled at some point in our lives. It can be hard to see the good in a situation that feels so bad. The trampling the potter does to the clay actually helps it. Not only does the trampling mix the clay, but it also removes air bubbles.

Potters seem to hang out in two different camps when it comes to asking them about air bubbles. One group believes air bubbles cause the piece to explode in the kiln. The trapped air will expand, causing the clay to burst apart. The second group says that residual moisture in the piece is the cause of explosions and that air bubbles have nothing to do with it; the only problem with an air bubble is the aesthetic defect it causes. I did some of my own testing to get to the bottom of this.

My personal conclusion is that if you have an air bubble in your clay, but your clay is completely bone dry, then the piece has a chance of not exploding. Likewise, if you have a piece that is relatively moist, but it does not have a single air bubble, the piece might have a chance of surviving the firing. This is where a long preheat in the kiln can sometimes save the kiln load. It's when moisture and air bubbles come together and reach water's boiling point to produce steam (expanded air) that a problem occurs. This expanded moisture in the clay will try to escape and evaporate in the hot kiln. Where does it go? That moisture goes straight into the air bubble on its way out. The air bubble, now filled with moisture, expands, and the piece explodes.

If you've never seen the aftermath of the explosion in a kiln, I've given you one of my own fine examples. The results are astounding. Usually the potter has to get a shop vacuum to clean all the tiny shards and debris out of all the nooks and crannies. Sometimes the exploding piece causes other pieces that were in the blast zone to break.

When I considered all this, I realized the air bubbles and moisture that create steam and cause problems in the kiln can symbolize jealousy, pride, and selfish judgment in our personal lives. They can hinder our usefulness in God's purpose. Little things can affect us and our neighbors in a big way if we do not give them to God and release our emotions surrounding them. If we harbor these "small," sinful feelings, they will come out in one way or another and can affect our relationships with God and with others. This "hot air" can cause explosions in our lives, wrecking relationships and limiting our witness. Ask God to help you work through these seemingly harmless flaws that end in large explosions and issues. As Isaiah says:

> "Seek the LORD while He may be found; call on Him while He is near. Let the wicked man forsake his own way and the unrighteous man his own thoughts; let him return to the LORD, that He may have compassion, and to our God, for He will freely pardon. For My thoughts are not your thoughts, neither are your ways My ways" (Isaiah 55:6-8).

Similar to the steam seething out of a piece in the kiln, potentially cracking the piece and damaging the kiln itself, our issues can be just as destructive, but God can provide the strength and self-control we need. It might be uncomfortable at first, but once our thoughts align with God's ways, our lives will become like wedged clay. The trampling will be uncomfortable, but it will save us and those around us. Our wants will align and flow with God's, and our air bubbles will get worked out of our lives. I find that when I am struggling with something and I don't know how to solve it, I just say Jesus's name. I call upon my Savior and ask for His control over the situation. It is amazing the miracles I've seen unfold in minor situations because I simply called out His name and truly, sincerely believed He would help me.

We are only human, and clay is only clay. Sometimes there are some hidden "air bubbles and moisture" that are hard to get out. We might feel squeezed or twisted, but God is right by our side, aiding and guiding us in His plan for our lives. God, the all-knowing Potter, meets us where we are and aids us in working through our tough times.

> "We are only human, and clay is only clay."

Wherever we are on our spiritual journeys, He prepares us for His plan. Lamentations 3 shows us this. The author, possibly Jeremiah, writes heart-wrenching verse after verse. He mourns that the Lord "has made my flesh and my skin waste away; he has broken my bones" (Lamentations 3:4). While these continuing metaphors are truly depressing, they also prophesy what is in store for Jesus Christ when he comes in the New Testament. This is a truth that Christians must find comfort in: Jesus experienced all of the hardships we face on earth . . . and He *overcame* them! Isn't that beautiful? Jesus chose to become the clay, a human being, so that humans would have a physical role model of how to live life on earth. Jesus knows our every struggle. He has personally faced each one *and* conquered them all. The author works through his sorrows to conclude that hope can be found in God.

God will again use clay to symbolize Old Testament prophecy. In Daniel 2, we read that the pagan king Nebuchadnezzar has asked Daniel to interpret yet another dream. In this dream, there is a human form made out of various metals, but the feet are "partly of iron and partly of clay" (Daniel 2:33). In the dream, a stone smashes the feet and the iron. Other metals and the clay go flying. Daniel interprets that Nebuchadnezzar's Kingdom will be overthrown and then another kingdom will rise to power after that. Daniel goes on to interpret the dream as foreshadowing the destruction of earthly kings and kingdoms, saying, "The God of heaven will set up a kingdom that shall never be destroyed" (Daniel 2:44).

Even clay and iron are weak compared to certain stones. Some potters will use tools coated in shards of diamonds to sand and finish their pots. The rock that smashes the clay and iron feet symbolizes God's might over earthly powers. In Psalm 18, David identifies and praises God as his strong rock. He says, "The LORD is my rock and my fortress and my deliverer, my God, my rock, in whom I take refuge" (Psalm 18:2). God is once again using clay to visualize His power and to foreshadow the hope that is to come for those who trust in Him.

From all we know about King Nebuchadnezzar, I conclude he was angry. I assume he might have been angry at David for his message; angry at the message itself; angry at the fate of his kingdom, and, mostly, angry at God for sending destruction. The end of Daniel Chapter 2 reveals that Nebuchadnezzar responded humbly. He bows before Daniel and commands an offering on his behalf. He promotes Daniel and recognizes God as ruler over all other earthly rulers. He even honors David's request and places Shadrach, Meshach, and Abednego in prominent positions. These are the same guys he later throws into a fiery furnace, maybe a pottery kiln. For that reason, they'll join us again in Chapter 11, but for now, they are enjoying the king's favor.

It seems clay is the bearer of bad news in both of these Old Testament prophecies. It's amazing how reading over them, we don't always catch how deeply meaningful the symbolism can be. God chooses His words carefully. He says and does exactly what He means and chooses to do. There is no coincidence that clay was used in these ways, for these specific verses. Now that we better understand the references, we can understand the verses more fully.

Creativity Challenge: David's Psalms and Nebuchadnezzar's dreams are filled with beautiful imagery. Poetically praise God this week. It can be as long as an epic poem or as short as a haiku. It can be a spoken word, or it might not have any words. Maybe you will choose to dance! Try to add some symbolism and metaphor to your poetry. This is just between you and God, so make it as personal and symbolic as you like. Try to throw in some beautiful imagery while you are at it!

This tool is my current signature stamp. It allows me to take ownership of my work by stamping each piece with my personally designed markings. It also allows collectors to know the authenticity of a piece. If a pot looks like my style but doesn't have my stamp, then it is not mine.

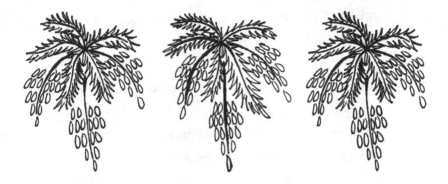

Chapter 7:

Gathering the Tools We Need

"All these things my hand has made, and so all these things came to be, declares the Lord. But this is the one to whom I will look: he who is humble and contrite in spirit and trembles at my word" (Isaiah 66:2).

"Nothing will be impossible with God" (Luke 1:37).

"Do not be conformed to this world, but be transformed by the renewal of your mind, that by testing you may discern what is the will of God, what is good and acceptable and perfect" (Romans 12:2).

"According to the grace of God given to me, like a skilled master builder I laid a foundation, and someone else is building upon it. Let each one take care how he builds upon it. For no one can lay a foundation other than that which is laid, which is Jesus Christ" (1 Corinthians 3:10-11).

"I have given them your word, and the world has hated them because they are not of the world, just as I am not of the world. I do not ask that you take them out of the world, but that you keep them from the evil one" (John 17:14-15).

We may not realize it, but we use tools every day. But we don't call them tools anymore. A tool can be anything that we use to make our jobs easier. Using a knife to cut vegetables in the kitchen counts as a tool. If you eat your food with a fork instead of your hands, that fork is a tool. If you are, in fact, eating with your hands, they are tools. A hair rubber band is a pretty useful tool at the gym. Look around you and you could probably find five tools laying in your line of vision. For me, I've got a spoon for the breakfast I am eating as I type these words. I have a pen for taking notes. The computer I'm typing on counts too. I've got a mug to hold my water. Number five is a clock that I keep glancing at to make sure I'm not late, although sometimes I still am.

Most ceramicists use their hands as their tools for making art. After all, hands are free, and for the most part, we can make them do what we want them to! There are tools we can use to help us as well. Tools come in a variety of sizes and forms, with some made to be used when the clay is wet and some made specifically for dry clay. There are wooden sculpting tools, wire-cutting tools, rubber rib tools, whisks, measuring cups, scales, drills, mixers, brushes, and others—all used in pottery. They are all useful in their own ways, so one cannot necessarily replace another.

A stamp is a type of tool that adds texture and design to a piece. There is a special kind of stamp, called a signature stamp, that allows the artist to make her mark on her piece. With this stamp, she takes ownership of her work. Her mark will be on the piece when it goes into the kiln. The artist's signature is on the piece before it feels the heat. Does this sound like symbolism? In the same way, a potter signs her work with a stamp, God signs His masterpieces. Don't believe me? Go back and reread Chapters 2 and 3!

Sometimes tools are handmade, while other times, tools are store-bought or even scavenged. The artist often decides what a tool is used for. Not all tools are the same. Some help guide the form of a piece on the wheel; others cut, carve, slice, extrude, or compress. Some tools take more clay away from the vessel than others. By removing clay, the vessel becomes lighter and more shapely. In the same way, we, as Christians, may carve down excess parts in our lives to streamline our walk with the Lord.

Some tools we have as Christians to help us in our daily lives are the Bible, the Church, and a fellowship of believers. Never underestimate the power of God's Word. Just reading a passage in the Bible can calm my anxious thoughts. It is the guidebook that tells us how to live our lives in a way that honors God. We can't do it alone, which is why the Church is so important. Getting connected to a local church strengthens your faith as you help to strengthen others. Serving in the Church is another great way to stay connected to God's will. Finally, a small friend group of believers is a great tool that can make all the difference in your faith. Having others hold you accountable is great, but having a safe space to ask hard questions is even better. Find people who you can be vulnerable with and allow yourselves to lean on each other as you walk by faith.

Pottery tools aren't just for the wheel, however. A free-standing slab roller is a timesaving tool when hand-building. It is essentially a table with rollers in the center that flatten clay to a desired thickness. It is easiest to set the roller to a large width and gradually tighten it, easing the slab into the desired thin width. Picture rolling out dough with a rolling pin. You ease the dough flat by rolling over it repeatedly.

One day, I was prepping for teaching a class, and I was in a time crunch. With the desire to save some time, I put a big block of clay into the slab roller at the desired thinness, thinking I'd just go from zero to sixty and get this thing done. Well, the crank wouldn't glide smoothly, and the clay bottlenecked at the rollers. I had to force it and pull it to wedge the large clay through the small slit. I got the thin slab, but it was wavy from going through the machine unevenly. You could see every pull I had made to get it through the rollers. The quality was not as good because I didn't allow the tool to work as it was designed.

I heard the Holy Spirit whisper to me. *This is what happens to your soul when you try to rush God's plan.* I try to push and pull my life along at breakneck speed to get to where I think I'm supposed to be, but that is not God's will. It takes time, and sometimes repetition, to change and learn from your surroundings. Just like the clay needed time in the machine to produce a perfectly flat slab, I needed time in the waiting season of my life. I couldn't see why, but there was something I needed to learn by staying and waiting in one place before moving on to the next step of my journey.

The Master Potter

God is the Master Potter. He is never embarrassed to call us His work of art. God declares in Isaiah 66:2, "All these things my hand has made, and so all these things came to be, declares the Lord. But this is the one to whom I will look: he who is humble and contrite in spirit and trembles at my word" (Isaiah 66:2). While Christians are not physically branded when they accept Jesus into their hearts and lives, the Holy Spirit does enter into their physical bodies and change them from the inside out. If you are a Christian, you are part of God's creation, and nothing can remove His stamp from you. It does not matter how you feel about your "design," God has chosen you and takes pride in you. You are His work; you are His creation.

I *know* this is hard! Ten years after my spinal fusion, I still struggle with body image. I know I'm not the only one who wishes she could change something about her appearance. It is a constant battle—I know it is—to block these negative thoughts out. I understand what I'm asking you (and myself) to do feels impossible, but "nothing will be impossible with God" (Luke 1:37). I have come to realize that when I can accept myself without judgment, it is

"You are His work; you are His creation."

easier for me to love and accept those around me as well. We must remember: "We are all the work of [His hands]" (Isaiah 64:8b). He allows us to spiritually mature before allowing another challenge to enter our lives. He gives us time and always helps us when we ask Him. He does not try to fix all our failures at once because he knows we might fall to pieces, like the clay. Instead, He is patient with us, helping us grow closer to Him over time.

Glorious Molds

Another type of tool used in pottery is a major part of the technique I use. Plaster molds are tools necessary for slip casting. The technique of slip casting is not as well-known as it used to be, but it is making a resurgence in the fine art niche of ceramics. I'll try to give you the quick rundown on slip casting without boring you too much!

To slip cast, you must begin with plaster molds. To make your plaster molds, you must start with a prototype. I make all of my prototypes by hand. Depending on what shape you are making a mold of, your mold might have to be two or more separate parts. I'll explain this more thoroughly at the end. You'll get your prototype, prep your pouring station, and mix your plaster. The plaster sets up quickly, so time is of the essence. Once you pour plaster into your mold form, you'll want to wait for it to dry completely. Plaster undergoes a chemical reaction when it is submerged in water and then agitated. When the plaster starts to set up, it will become hot to the touch. Once it has hardened, it will cool down.

Then you can take the mold form and prototype off of your plaster. You should be left with the negative representation of the item that is your prototype. Of course, there will be a hole at one end for you to pour your clay into. Speaking of which, time to mix up some slip! The term *slip* refers to clay that has been turned into a pourable consistency. Additional water and deflocculates are added to the clay, causing the clay particles to be suspended in water.

Pour the slip into the hole in the top of the mold, then fill the mold until the slip is level with the top of the mold. The plaster is porous and dry, so it will absorb the extra moisture that was added to the clay. As the slip dries inside the mold, you'll notice a ring of clay building up around the contact point with the plaster. It is creating a shell, molded to the exact design you had made in the plaster. Once the ring is thick enough, pour out the rest of the slip. Now, you have a perfect shell of your design. This is called the *cast*. It has been cast with slip from the mold you made of plaster, hence "slip casting."

Once the piece has dried out enough that it will hold its own shape, it is time to remove it from the plaster mold. This step requires a gentle touch. You are handling a fragile piece of clay. Remember the part about the different number of pieces for the mold? That comes back into play here. To get the clay cast out freely, you must be able to move it in a way that it won't get hung. For example, your coffee mug with a handle would most likely take a two-part mold so you could put the seam down the handle and pull it apart from the two sides. If it has a handle and a foot, it would need a three-part mold. You can have as many parts to a mold as you want. The beauty in the mold making is being able to use the molds over and over again, getting almost identical products, until the plaster molds wear out.

Conforming

Paul challenges us in Romans, "Do not be conformed to this world, but be transformed by the renewal of your mind, that by testing you may discern what is the will of God, what is good and acceptable and perfect" (Romans 12:2). This verse is powerful, as the slip naturally *conforms* to the mold. The plaster traps and forces it into that specific shape. The deflocculates in the clay allow the clay to remain in a fluid state. It is a liquid, filling any container it flows into. Clay that has not been converted to slip is moist and malleable but will not flow into any container. If you put a ball of clay in a bucket, it might sag on the bottom, but it is still a ball of clay. It is susceptible to change, but it can also hold its own.

Spiritually, we must be like the clay and not like the slip. God's word must be our foundation. We must ground ourselves in the truth of Jesus Christ. He smashes the plaster molds of the world. Why should we still try to loosen our morals to fit into the rigid molds of this world? We know that fame is fleeting. Think of the number of awards shows that will be on television this year. These are *annual* awards shows. That means each year, there's a *new* best famous person. Every year. But there isn't just one famous person; there are many contests. This culture cranks out famous people and then has no problem dropping or canceling them and moving on.

If we see Jesus Christ as the foundation for our lives . . . "no one can lay a foundation other than that which is laid, which is Jesus Christ" (1 Corinthians 3:11). Only one foundation is laid for building a house. You can't build a foundation on top of another foundation. If God's Word is truly our foundation for every decision in life, then the world's morals can't phase us; we have already been grounded in the faith. We are like the ball of clay in the bucket instead of the slip. We can stand alone because we are not alone.

The Bible is one of the best tools we as Christians have in standing against this world in our faith. Jesus commands us to remain *in the world* to evangelize, but not to be *of the world* in spirit. He prays to God, "I have given them your word, and the world has hated them because they are not of the world, just as I am not of the world" (John 17:14). The Bible is to be our guiding tool in the lives we must live until Jesus calls us home or comes back.

> "We can stand alone because we are not alone."

Remember, the Bible is not our only tool. There are videos, study aids, books, podcasts, sermons, small groups, and more. All of these things, including (most importantly) the Holy Spirit, can be tools we can utilize to help us in our walks with Christ. People in our lives can be tools for good or for bad, and so can we.

Creativity Challenge: Think of a tool that makes your job easier. It could be a pencil sharpener, a calculator, a washing machine, an alarm clock—you get the picture. Now consider trying to do your job without that tool. Everything would be much harder, right? Similarly, living our lives without the tools God has given us makes our spiritual walk all the more challenging. This week, do something nice for your fellowship of believers! Maybe send a card to your small group leader; mail a handwritten prayer to a struggling Christian friend; make cookies for your Sunday School members—the sky's the limit!

The clay is centered when it feels equally smooth underneath your hands.
If your hands are wobbling back and forth on the wheel,
then the clay isn't quite centered yet

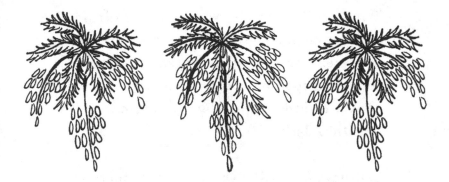

Chapter 8:

Centering and Being Centered

"Do not swerve to the right or to the left; turn your foot away from evil" (Proverbs 4:27).

"For the gate is narrow and the way is hard that leads to life, and those who find it are few" (Matthew 7:14).

"But God's firm foundation stands, bearing this seal: 'The Lord knows those who are his,' and, 'Let everyone who names the name of the Lord depart from iniquity'" (2 Timothy 2:19).

"But when he saw the wind, he was afraid, and beginning to sink he cried out, 'Lord, save me.' Jesus immediately reached out his hand and took hold of him, saying to him, 'O you of little faith, why did you doubt?'" (Matthew 14:30-31).

"But now, O LORD, you are our Father; we are the clay, and you are our potter; we are all the work of your hand" (Isaiah 64:8).

"All things were made through him, and without him was not any thing made that was made" (John 1:3).

"Thus says the Lord GOD: This is Jerusalem. I have set her in the center of the nations, with countries all around her. And she has rebelled against my rules by doing wickedness more than the nations, and against my statutes more than the countries all around her; for they have rejected my rules and have not walked in my statutes" (Ezekiel 5:5-6).

'm sure you're familiar with the concept of throwing clay on a pottery wheel. It seems to be the glamorous part of pottery that makes it into the media. Movies, television shows, and even medication commercials all seem to showcase someone who is just messy enough, throwing clay on the wheel. Usually, her hair is falling out of a bun, and she has one swipe of clay across her forehead. The clay is (magically) spinning perfectly in the center of the wheel, and her slightly clay-stained hands are resting on it in a calming Zen kind of moment.

Just like with other skilled activities, learning to throw takes work. It takes time, and it takes patience. When throwing clay on a pottery wheel, the main goal is to center the clay and keep it centered for the entire time. Centered clay sits perfectly in the center of the wheel; it doesn't wobble from side to side.

Have you ever watched dancers twirl and spin? I love to watch ice dancing when the Olympic games are on television. The dancer must be perfectly balanced into her body's center of gravity; otherwise, she will bobble and could fall out of her turn. To take full advantage of that centripetal force, the artist must create radial symmetry around the axis, or the center. This same idea applies to wheel throwing.

When the clay starts to wobble from right to left, the artist must place her hands firmly on the clay to steady it. Her arms must be the constant stable force to keep the clay centered. Her body should be positioned so that the waist aligns with the wheel head. Her back should be straight and leaning over the wheel. The upper arms through the elbows and forearms should be tight and bracing. She can be standing or sitting, depending on the wheel. The hands are constantly feeling and responding. The clay will bend and form around the hands and will eventually become centered. Sometimes, the potter must apply the force of her entire body as well as use leverage techniques to move the clay into a centered state. When the potter becomes the firm foundation and holds herself steady, the clay will physically conform to her commands.

As a young (and not overly strong) potter, I could not always get my clay completely centered. Part of this problem also comes from my impatient streak. I wouldn't keep at the clay until I felt it stabilize in the center of the wheel head. I wanted to rush ahead to the more fun aspects of shaping the pot. I learned quickly that if I rushed the clay and moved on to the next steps too soon, I would usually end up completely destroying my piece. If I decided to pull the walls before the clay was centered, I would have a very wobbly vessel. If I wanted to trim the piece before it had dried enough, I'd end up making holes in the wet clay or the piece would simply just fly off of the wheel and crumple on the floor.

If the clay is not centered, the walls of the pot on the wheel will be uneven. One side will be thin, while the other will be thick. This leads to a poorly made pot and could result in cracking or the complete loss of the piece. Beginners on the wheel can't help but start a bit off center. It takes practice to learn the feel of centered clay and to know how to get it there.

If we look at Proverbs 4, we can apply this lesson spiritually as well. "Do not swerve to the right or to the left; turn your foot away from evil" (Proverbs 4:27). When we don't follow God's will, our desires pull us off of alignment. God will no longer be the center of our life, and this will make us wobble in this world. We must stop swerving away from God's desires and remember where our focus should lie. We can't choose both the right and left paths.

We must focus on God's straight plan. Jesus tells us in Matthew 7, ". . . the gate is narrow and the way is hard that leads to life, and those who find it are few" (Matthew 7:14). It is easy to be off-centered. You can throw off-centered clay on the wheel without trying. There are many ways for us to be off-centered too. You can be almost centered or really far gone, but both classify as being out of alignment. Centering is not just for the wheel! We must also center our spiritual lives on the ways of the Lord.

When working three-dimensionally, balance and gravity are huge contributors. Clay must be handled in a structurally sound way. Otherwise, disaster can happen. When throwing something like a wide bowl or a plate, the potter must be sure to pay attention to how wet the clay is becoming. Experience and practice are key for the potter. If the potter uses too much water or is not quick enough, gravity and the softness of the clay can cause the walls to fall apart. Beginners are taught to throw cylinders for this reason. When throwing cylinders on the pottery wheel, the focus is on making the walls even. The artist is less concerned with the design and more concerned with the construction of the form. Throwing cylinders trains the potter's hands to adjust to the centripetal force of the clay moving on the pottery wheel. The thinner the clay is pulled, the more risky it can be to alter its shape. If the base and the walls are not similar in thickness, the base or walls might crack. Again, it is key to have a firm, centered foundation.

We must rely on God to help center us! Clay cannot center itself. It can't even turn the wheel on! If you placed a round ball of clay in the center of the wheel and then turned the wheel on, that clay would fly right off. It would not be centered because the potter had not touched it. The potter must do the work, but the clay must be in a soft enough state to be receptive to it. That is what we, as Christians, must do; we must soften our hearts and ourselves so we can be receptive to God's work in our lives.

God is our firm foundation. Paul writes to Timothy, explaining, "God's firm foundation stands, bearing this seal: 'The Lord knows those who are his,' and, 'Let everyone who names the name of the Lord depart from iniquity'" (2 Timothy 2:19). This imagery God provides of Himself as the potter and His children as the clay proves exceedingly beautiful here. When we falter, when we choose to disobey, when we doubt, or when we sin, we become like the off-centered clay; our focus is no longer on God.

We are like Peter trying to walk on water in Matthew 14:29; when he sees the storms, he takes his eyes off Jesus—his foundation—and sinks. We become wobbly in our own beliefs, no longer able to hold on to truth. BUT GOD! God is our solid footing. He is that steady arm that guides us back into place. Matthew tells us that as soon as Peter cried out to God, "Jesus immediately reached out his hand and took hold of him, saying to him, 'O you of little faith, why did you doubt?'" (Matthew 14:31). Truth can be found through His Word and can be used to "center" our lives.

Just like the clay on the wheel, if we are not centered in God's truth, we will be "off-centered" Christians. Our lives, like the walls of the off-centered pots, will be uneven. A hard thing I am still learning is that a Christian cannot be afraid and trust in God at the same time. Fear is not knowing what is to come, but God knows all. Fear is feeling helpless, but God is in control. The danger comes when we, as Christians, stay in the off-centered phase. We go to church or say the right things, but our actions are not aligned with our words. Our motives are off. It is crucial that we regain our focus on God through His help.

When we feel afraid, it is comforting to remember that we are not in control. We are merely the clay that God uses. Our prayer to God should be from Isaiah; "But now, O LORD, you are our Father, we are the clay, and you are our potter; we are all the work of your hand" (Isaiah 64:8). Like the clay on the wheel, we must be willing to change, sometimes drastically, to remain centered in Christ. God is the unchanging Potter whose strong hands guide us, however firmly, to His will. He is the ultimate Creator. "All things were made through him, and without him was not any thing made that was made" (John 1:3). Find comfort in the truth that God Himself chose to make you. He took the time and effort to design this entire universe, from the widest expanses to the smallest cells. Nothing goes unnoticed by Him.

The word *center* isn't found too often in the Bible. Ezekiel records God using the word: "Thus says the Lord God: This is Jerusalem. I have set her in the center of the nations, with countries all around her" (Ezekiel 5:5). God put Jerusalem in the center to be a guiding light for surrounding nations. Like our lives being centered around God, Jerusalem was supposed to remain in the center of God's will like the eye of a hurricane. Jerusalem should remain calm and focused on God while the craziness of the world wobbled and spiraled off-center. Instead, God says, "She has rebelled against my rules by doing wicked-ness more than the nations, and against my statutes more than the countries all around her; for they have rejected my rules and have not walked in my statutes" (Ezekiel 5:6). The people of Jerusalem have given into the world's temptations, and even though they are physically centered in the midst of nations, they are just as wobbly as everyone else.

God's judgment will come as a disaster for Jerusalem. God allows her to be destroyed because she did not keep God at her center. Has this ever happened to you? Was there ever a time you realized everything was rocking to and fro because God wasn't the center of your life anymore? Sometimes, we knowingly push Him aside and do what we want to, anyway. Other times, it sneaks up on us. We think we are putting God first, but we have lost the feel of our lives being centered around God.

We become so used to the wobbling of the world that it rocks us into a false feeling of security. When I was about to graduate college, I wanted to move straight into the perfect full-time job. I had found several perfect jobs in neat cities that seemed well-suited to move to; the only issue was that the companies didn't see *me* as the perfect candidate. I felt defeated, especially since most of my friends had gotten jobs and were moving away. I ended up moving back home that summer and doing some odd jobs. Finally, in October, I got what was, for a while, my dream job.

If I had gotten the original jobs in event planning that I had wanted, I would have been laid off less than a year later because of the pandemic. The Lord definitely protected me then, just as He does now and will do in the future.

How easy it is to make our wants and needs the center of our lives and attention. I thought I was following God by trying to get a job straight out of college. I'm not saying this is wrong, but God was saying it was the wrong timing for me. I was seeking what the world told me was necessary to do so I wouldn't be a failure. That summer, I was able to move past the crippling anxiety I had developed in college. If I had gone straight into a job the Lord hadn't wanted me to take, who knows? My anxiety may have grown even more dangerous.

Take time to truly seek God's will for your life. The Bible guides us with practical rules for Christians to follow. Pay specific attention to those words in red. Jesus's recorded words teach us so much about how to live and how to love others as God intended. Don't underestimate the value of prayer, either. If it is hard for you to close your eyes and pray in silence, consider prayer journaling. I have found that writing my prayers to God like a letter helps me see and organize my thoughts. They aren't for anyone else but God and me to read. Seek after Him today to stop the wobbling and get centered in His plan.

Creativity Challenge: How would you define being centered in Christ? Grab two pieces of paper, a writing utensil, a dowel, and some string. First, try freehand drawing a perfectly round circle. Don't use any aids, just try to make a perfect circle. Now get the second piece of paper. Tie a knot in the string to make a loop. Place your dowel in the center of the paper and wrap your string around both the dowel and the writing utensil. With one hand, hold the dowel still, with the other hand, move the writing utensil around the dowel, being restricted by the string. Now compare the two circles. I'm sure the second circle is a lot closer to perfection. God is that dowel and string that hold us toward His center. Write everything that centers you in your faith in the second circle and fill the first circle with distractions.

I am able to remove excess clay from the base of my piece and create a foot by using this metal ribbon trimming tool. While the clay turns on the wheel once again, I apply my tool and watch the clay shave off.

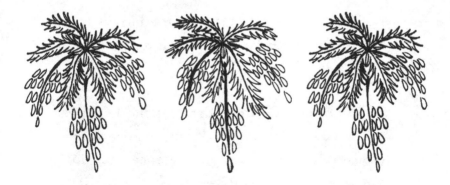

Chapter 9:

Trimming It All Down

"Do not be unequally yoked with unbelievers. For what partnership has righteousness with lawlessness? Or what fellowship has light with darkness?" (2 Corinthians 6:14).

"Remove vexation from your heart, and put away pain from your body, for youth and the dawn of life are vanity" (Ecclesiastes 11:10).

"Wash yourselves; make yourselves clean; remove the evil of your deeds from before my eyes; cease to do evil, learn to do good;

seek justice, correct oppression; bring justice to the fatherless, plead the widow's cause" (Isaiah 1:16-17).

"If you return, O Israel, declares the LORD, to me you should return. If you remove your detestable things from my presence, and do not waver, and if you swear, 'As the LORD lives,' in truth, in justice, and in righteousness, then nations shall bless themselves in him, and in him shall they glory" (Jeremiah 4:1-2).

"And the son said to him, 'Father, I have sinned against heaven and before you. I am no longer worthy to be called your son.' But the father said to his servants, 'Bring quickly the best robe, and put it on him, and put a ring on his hand, and shoes on his feet. And bring the fattened calf and kill it, and let us eat and celebrate. For this my son was dead, and is alive again; he was lost, and is found.' And they began to celebrate" (Luke 15:21-24).

"But he was angry and refused to go in. His father came out and entreated him, but he answered his father, 'Look, these many years I have served you, and I never disobeyed your command, yet you never gave me a young goat, that I might celebrate with my friends" (Luke 15:28-30).

"And he said to him, 'Son, you are always with me and all that is mine is yours, It was fitting to celebrate and be glad, for this your brother was dead, and is alive; he was lost, and is found'" (Luke 15:31-32).

"And if your eye causes you to sin, tear it out and throw it away. It is better for you to enter life with one eye than with two eyes to be thrown into the hell of fire" (Matthew 18:9).

"Woe to him who strives with him who formed him, a pot among earthen pots! Does the clay say to him who forms it, 'What are you making?' or 'Your work has no handles'?" (Isaiah 45:9).

"You turn things upside down! Shall the potter be regarded as the clay, that the thing made should say of its maker, 'He did not make me'; or the thing formed say of him who formed it, 'He has no understanding?'" (Isaiah 29:16).

Getting a haircut, losing some weight, quitting a bad habit, and cleaning out a closet are all ways we naturally trim down ourselves and our lives. We get to a point where we realize our lives would be better if we lost the excess. Sometimes, it is painless and easy, while at other times, it can lead to drastic life adjustments.

Similarly, trimming allows ceramic work to be streamlined and cleaned up before firing. During trimming, clay is subtracted from the form. As the excess clay is removed, the silhouette of the vessel is realized. Craftsmanship plays a key role in finishing the piece. Trimming most commonly occurs on the wheel but can also be done by hand carving, faceting, or rasping. Trimming on the wheel can be especially mesmerizing, watching slivers of clay spin off of the vessel while its silhouette changes.

There are several ways to go about trimming in the pottery world. The one you are probably most familiar with would be trimming on the wheel. The potter re-centers her pot upside down on the wheel and uses sharp tools (usually made of metal) to shave clay away as the pot is turning. This is similar to wood working on a lathe. You can also trim by using rasping tools. These tools work similarly to cheese graters. The potter holds the clay stationary (no pottery wheel required) and scrapes off the clay. You can carve clay just as you would carve wood, soap, or stone. You can also facet clay by using a taut wire to slice clay off. After the piece has been trimmed, some surface decoration might be added or handles may be attached, but when trimming, only subtraction occurs.

Sometimes we need to do some trimming in our lives too. And in some cases, God does the trimming for us. Paul's advice to "not be unequally yoked with unbelievers" can bring about some trimming in our lives (2 Corinthians 6:14). Think of a team of animals trying to pull a cart together; they have to be of the same strength. If you pair a miniature pony with an ox, the animals will pull unevenly, and the cart will not move smoothly. If two people do not share the same faith, then their relationship can struggle because they most likely will not share the same values and priorities. This verse is usually considered in the context of marriage, but it can be applied to most relationships, including business relationships. Notice Paul is not talking about completely separating from non-believers. He believed in evangelism. He is talking about people with different values trying to do life together. If you struggle with a certain sin, like drunkenness, then it would not be wise for you and your friends to meet in bars. They would not be good friends if they put their entertainment above your struggles.

Christians and non-Christians will likely have different viewpoints on some issues, and it will be challenging to agree. The relationship will be like an off-centered pot flailing around on the wheel. Off-centered pots rarely make it to the finished state because of all the problems and potential cracking that can occur. And uneven pots are challenging to trim. One side is thicker than the other, meaning that when the piece is put back on the wheel to trim, it can't get centered (since it never was), and if one is not careful, the thin spots will get even thinner until the trimming tool punches through the piece altogether.

The Bible instructs us to trim the sin and worldly desires from our lives. In Ecclesiastes, God tells us to "remove vexation from your heart, and put away pain from your body, for youth and the dawn of life are vanity" (Ecclesiastes 11:10). The author of Ecclesiastes warns that when we are young, we feel invincible. We believe we can do things that will have no lasting consequences. This verse reminds us that we should separate ourselves from the dangers of the world as early as possible. It calls out anyone who believes their actions won't have consequences—including teenagers, typically vain in their thinking. This verse takes trimming very seriously. If we leave little issues unaddressed when we are young, they grow into bigger issues and are much harder to remove from our adulthood.

In Isaiah, we get more instruction as to how we should go about trimming the ungodly from our lives. God, through Isaiah, tells His people to "wash yourselves; make yourselves clean; remove the evil of your deeds from before my eyes; cease to do evil, learn to do good; seek justice, correct oppression; bring justice to the fatherless, plead the widow's cause" (Isaiah 1:16–17). Instead of living as the world lives, we should trim away our distractions and focus our attention on God. He suggests helping others who are struggling too. I'm sure you've heard the saying that the best way to make yourself feel better is to help others, and this verse reflects that. When you make someone else smile or move toward more godliness, you feel good too!

The thing about trimming is that if it is done correctly, the piece looks so much better than before. A piece that has not been trimmed is usually a lot heavier at the base than it looks. The weight of the clay settles at the base, and it can become hard to remove. If all of this clay is left on the piece, the weight is off balance, compared to how the piece looks. I had a teacher who would warn us about such "dishonest" pots.

She would tell us that our pots must be trimmed to feel as heavy or as light as they look. If the pot is heavier than it looks, the buyer will recognize this as poor craftsmanship. No one wants a mug that gives you an arm workout just drinking your coffee. Similarly, if the piece is over trimmed, the pot will weigh less than it looks. This is also bad. If a piece is trimmed too thin, it becomes fragile. A serving platter that is too light will snap under the weight of the food it is holding. Obviously, this is not ideal either. We must have honest pots—ones that look as heavy as they feel. We want pots that can do the job they were designed to perform.

Again, God warns His people in Jeremiah to trim away their sinful ways and return to Him. He says, "If you remove your detestable things from my presence, and do not waver, and if you swear, 'As the LORD lives,' in truth, in justice, and in righteousness, then nations shall bless themselves in him, and in him shall they glory" (Jeremiah 4:1–2). God promises glory to those who can trim away their temptations.

It can be a challenge to trim spiritually and correctly on the pottery wheel but it's worth it.

Some potters love to trim, and others hate it. Those who love trimming will purposefully leave themselves enough clay to successfully trim intricate feet. The foot of the piece is the bottom ring the piece sits on. The potters who don't love trimming try to get the piece as close to finished as possible when throwing. That way, they don't have to trim as much later on. Both ways are acceptable, and I believe this applies to our spiritual lives as well.

Consider the prodigal son. He sought worldly pleasures, but when he realized his mistake, he trimmed them away to be with his father again. He is like the pot that is weighed down with clay; it all must be removed for him to be in his father's presence again. "And the son said to him, 'Father, I have sinned against heaven and before you. I am no longer worthy to be called your son'" (Luke 15:21). The son recognized his mistakes. He left his sinful life and returned home.

The father received him gratefully. "The father said to his servants, 'Bring quickly the best robe, and put it on him, and put a ring on his hand, and shoes on his feet. And bring the fattened calf and kill it, and let us eat and celebrate. For this my son was dead, and is alive again; he was lost, and is found.' And they began to celebrate" (Luke 15:22–24). In the end, it didn't matter how much had to be removed; it only mattered that the son was willing to remove it. The overjoyed father was grateful for his return.

The second son is like the pot thrown with little excess clay. He never left his father to seek worldly gain. He was diligent with his father's work. He became upset with how happy his father was . . . "He was angry and refused to go in. His father came out and entreated him, but he answered his father, 'Look, these many years I have served you, and I never disobeyed your command, yet you never gave me a young goat, that I might celebrate with my friends'" (Luke 15:28–30). He thought he should have been treated better because he never needed as much trimming. The father explained, "Son, you are always with me and all that is mine is yours. It was fitting to celebrate and be glad, for this your brother was dead, and is alive; he was lost, and is found" (Luke 15:31–32). The father recognized that his dutiful son didn't need as much trimming, but he was not flawless. The son's feelings of resentment highlight an issue the first son can't seem to see in himself. He still needs to trim that sin out of his life.

Both sons were unworthy, but the father graciously saw the value in each of them. He acknowledged them both as his sons and provided for both of their needs. Both types of pots are beautiful in their final results. The buyer never sees how little or how much was trimmed. It doesn't matter how much you must remove; all that matters is that you are willing to remove it!

Sometimes, the trimming God chooses to perform is on the external things in our lives, and sometimes, it is with the internal. We, as Christians, are responsible for our actions, so we need to make the decision to trim off the bad distractions in our lives. Jesus says, "And if your eye causes you to sin, tear it out and throw it away. It is better for you to enter life with one eye than with two eyes to be thrown into the hell of fire" (Matthew 18:9). This dramatic visual gives a good example of the dangers of sin. The Bible tells us that we must do our best to completely remove, or trim off, anything that provokes us to sin. It can be hard to look at yourself and wonder why God chooses to send certain things your way. I mentioned earlier that I had scoliosis surgery while in middle school. The surgery was necessary for my body to function correctly, but I could not seem to get past my negative body image and physical limitations. More than ten years post-surgery, I am still fighting those negative thoughts, but I am not alone.

I am not alone in two different ways. The first way is that I know you also struggle with God over something He has allowed to happen to you or in your life. I know this because as far back in history as the time of Isaiah, these struggles have been recorded. The Prophet Isaiah warns, "Woe to him who strives with him who formed him, a pot among earthen pots! Does the clay say to him who forms it, 'What are you making?' or 'Your work has no handles'?" (Isaiah 45:9). Yes it is my life, but God is the Artist who created me and gave me that life. Who am I to question how or why He did what He did?

As God's creation, my job is to point back to Him. I should praise Him for making me instead of complaining to Him about how He chose to make me. The part about the handles does crack me up a little. Not all ceramic pots need handles. Look at Asian tea culture! Or better yet, open up your cabinet and pull out your cereal bowl and your dinner plate. I use these things every day, and if I'm lucky and actually sit down for all three meals, I use them multiple times a day! Imagine a plate having handles. First of all, the handles would be rather useless. Second, they would break off when you loaded your dishwasher, rendering that beautiful plate damaged and useless.

Why should I dare to question how God made me? He made me exactly how He wanted me to be made. He is the Perfect Potter; it is completely against His nature to make me imperfectly—His design can't be flawed! It's a little hard to wrap my brain around, but it's true because everything in the Bible is true. Isaiah gives us a stern talking to by asking, "Shall the potter be regarded as the clay, that the thing made should say of its maker, 'He did not make me'; or the thing formed say of him who formed it, 'He has no understanding?'" (Isaiah 29:16). When I am in my studio, I recognize that although it can feel like the clay has a mind of its own, it truly has no authority over me or my decisions. I am the one working with it. I know what I intend to make, and I am in control, using my hands and tools to shape the clay into what I choose for it to be.

I must recognize this relationship and reverse my role in it for my relationship with my God. I become the clay. I have no authority over God's decisions. God is the one working with me. God knows what He intends to make out of my life, and He is in control, using His power to shape me into what He chooses for me to be. To some extent, I'll be learning this lesson my entire life, but the sooner I can wrap my head around it and give God the control in my life that He already has, the easier it will be for me to trust in Him completely.

Creativity Challenge: What is something in your life that you try to hold complete control over? It might be your weight, your schedule, your future plans, or your finances. Find a way to creatively make something that represents your control over that aspect of your life, then give it to God. Maybe write it on a balloon, then pop it, or mold a piece of cotton candy and dissolve it in water, or write down a list and (safely) burn it. Whatever representation you choose, relinquish control over your life and allow God to be the all-powerful Creator He already is.

I let my clay scraps dry out in a bucket so I can reuse them.
Once the clay is completely dry, I'll add water to slake the clay down
into a smooth slurry mixture, then I'll process that back into workable clay.

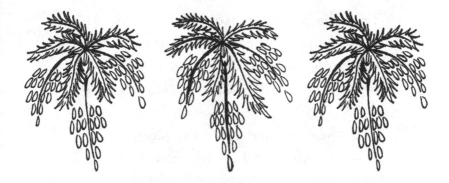

Chapter 10:

Drying Out and Living Water

"I am poured out like water, and all my bones are out of joint; my heart is like wax, it is melted within my breast; my strength is dried up like a potsherd, and my tongue sticks to my jaws; you lay me in the dust of death" (Psalm 22:14-15).

"Jesus answered her, 'If you knew the gift of God, and who it is that is saying to you, "Give me a drink," you would have asked him, and he would have given you living water'" (John 4:10).

"Then the magicians said to Pharaoh, 'This is the finger of God.' But Pharaoh's heart was hardened, and he would not listen to them, as the LORD had said" (Exodus 8:19).

"And Pharaoh rose up in the night, he and all his servants and all the Egyptians. And there was a great cry in Egypt, for there was not a house where someone was not dead. Then he summoned Moses and Aaron by night and said, 'Up, go out from among my people, both you and the people of Israel; and go, serve the LORD, as you have said, Take your flocks and your herds, as you have said, and be gone, and bless me also!'" (Exodus 12:30-32).

"Blessed is the one who fears the LORD always, but whoever hardens his heart will fall into calamity" (Proverbs 28:14).

"Whoever believes in me, as the Scripture has said, 'Out of his heart will flow rivers of living water'" (John 7:38).

"Therefore, if anyone is in Christ, he is a new creation. The old has passed away; behold, the new has come" (2 Corinthians 5:17).

"Beware lest there be among you a man or woman or clan or tribe whose heart is turning away today from the LORD our God to go and serve the gods of those nations. Beware lest there be among you a root bearing poisonous and bitter fruit, one who, when he hears the words of this sworn covenant, blesses himself in his heart, saying, 'I shall be safe, though I walk in the stubbornness of my heart.' This will lead to the sweeping away of moist and dry alike" (Deuteronomy 29:18-20).

"Create in me a clean heart, O God; and renew a right spirit within me" (Psalm 51:10).

"O God, you are my God; earnestly I seek you; my soul thirsts for you; my flesh faints for you, as in a dry and weary land where there is no water" (Psalm 63:1).

"For I will pour water on the thirsty land, and streams on the dry ground; I will pour my Spirit upon your offspring, and my blessing on your descendants" (Isaiah 44:3).

"Draw near to God, and he will draw near to you. Cleanse your hands, you sinners, and purify your hearts, you double-minded" (James 4:8).

t is pretty well known that without water, living things will die. People who know me well will probably laugh upon reading that statement because I tend to carry around a water bottle that I never seem to drink. I admit, it is not a wise way to live. Living things must stay hydrated, or they will die (Medical News Today). Some of the more common side effects of dehydration include headaches, sluggishness, dry skin, and weak muscles. That is not good, my friends. Have you ever forgotten to water a plant? It doesn't take long for that plant to start looking wilted. Just as lack of water can harm our physical bodies, missing out on the Living Water that Jesus provides puts our souls in danger.

The psalmist gives us some pretty intense imagery, writing, "My strength is dried up like a potsherd, and my tongue sticks to my jaws; you lay me in the dust of death" (Psalm 22:15b). The author cries out to God in despair. He accuses God of leaving him in his moment of weakness. He needs God's grace and Living Water to flow within him, but he feels abandoned and dry of all hope. This is a perfect comparison to physical dehydration *and* to bone-dry clay, which we will get to in a bit. This chapter in the Psalms is thought to foreshadow Jesus's death, when God must turn away from His only Son who has taken on all sin of the world.

Jesus tells the Samaritan woman at the well that if she knew who she was talking to, she would be asking Him, "And he would have given (her) living water" (John 4:10b). Our faith in Jesus as the Lord and Savior of our lives is the water to our souls; He allows us to be refreshed in Him and live forever. Consider these next paragraphs as symbols because that is what God has made them. Wherever you see references to *clay*, replace them with your life. When you read about water and moisture, picture the Living Water of Jesus that gives us eternal life.

Intermittently, throughout creating, the potter must check the stages of the clay. There are three stages of drying: wet greenware, leather hard, and bone dry. All three of these stages technically fall under the umbrella of greenware because they have not undergone the heat of a bisque firing yet.

When comparing Christians to clay, wet, workable clay is the most desirable stage to be in. This is before it has even started drying to become greenware. Our hearts are open and willing to allow God to do His work. We are receptive to the Holy Spirit within us and allow God to shape us into His design for our lives. We are willing to change for Christ.

Wet clay is very malleable. At this stage, the clay is perfect for constructing. It leaves a moist residue on the surface it touches because the water within it makes it soft. Wet clay can adjust to the most drastic formations here because it is very pliable and responds well to the potter's touch. It has the possibility of becoming anything the artist decides for it to be.

Leather hard clay feels like stiff leather. The leather hard stage is where the clay has started setting up and drying out. It has begun to dry but is still damp. It is smooth and cool, but not wet to the touch. At this stage, the clay is sturdy enough to take some alteration, but is not wet enough to be altered significantly. The clay is sturdy and holds its shape well.

At the leather hard Christian stage, we are still doing and saying everything correctly, but we have taken our focus off of God. We are uncentered, not focusing on God's Kingdom, which is the end goal. Our relationship with the Almighty Potter is struggling. This reflects the image of a closed-minded Christian. This person has followed all the rules but is unwilling to take the leap of faith and obey God's bigger requests. The clay toughens because it loses the water it needs to stay soft. The closed-minded Christian has lost some of the freshness of Living Water.

Techniques like carving, trimming, surface decoration, adding handles, and cleaning up sharp edges work best at this stage. The clay can still be manipulated and altered, but it will not handle big changes well. It is becoming rigid, conformed to the shape it is in because the clay is no longer holding onto the water. Leather hard clay can also become brittle toward the end of the drying cycle. If not handled carefully, the clay could crack, attachments might fall off, and uneven drying could lead to warping.

Bone dry clay is exactly what it sounds like—clay that is completely dry. There is no water in the clay at all at this stage. The clay feels dry and chalky to the touch. Clay dust comes off onto one's hands. The clay no longer feels cold or damp from moisture. It is also lighter in color because of the absence of water. At this stage, the only thing that can be done to the clay is sanding (with a mask so you don't breathe in the dry particles). If the clay is bumped at this stage, it is so brittle that it will break. If the piece is dropped, it will shatter. The clay is not malleable in any way.

Bone dry Christians are set in their ways. They can be too stubborn to let God have any power in their lives. They might have been willing to change at one point, but now they can't be swayed in their opinions and are not necessarily listening to

God's voice. Of course, God still loves His creation, but unless the person is willing to accept the Living Water of the Holy Spirit back into her life, it will seem nearly impossible to change.

The imagery of the different characteristics between the soft and hard clay calls to memory all the times God softened or hardened someone's heart in the Bible. For instance, God hardens Pharaoh's heart in Exodus 7–12 to bring glory to Himself and strengthen the faith of the Israelites.

God sends ten plagues upon Egypt, proving to Pharaoh that the God of the Israelites is the only God. You would think after a couple of plagues, Pharaoh would call it quits. Right at the moment we think he might change his mind, "Pharaoh's heart was hardened, and he would not listen to them, as the LORD had said" (Exodus 8:19). This continues through the plagues of the Nile filled with blood, frogs, gnats, flies, the death of Egyptian livestock, boils and sores, hail, locusts, and darkness. That is nine plagues of grossness. Nine times God has proven who is really in charge, and nine times Pharaoh has tried to be in control.

The tenth plague kills the firstborn living thing in every household where The Passover did not take place. This included people and animals who did not listen to God. After this plague, Pharaoh's heart has shattered. His hard heart had become brittle and then, as a consequence, crushed. In the middle of the night, Pharaoh "summoned Moses and Aaron by night and said, 'Up, go out from among my people, both you and the people of Israel; and go, serve the LORD, as you have said, Take your flocks and your herds, as you have said, and be gone, and bless me also!'" (Exodus 12:30–32). Pharaoh's heart became like bone-dry clay.

He did not have the Living Water of God's love to soften it, so it became brittle and unyielding. He openly rejected God and therefore rejected the love, grace, and understanding that come with the Holy Spirit. He did not have the spiritual motivation to soften his heart to forgiveness and understanding.

If we are not saturated in a relationship with Jesus and in God's Word, we will become like the bone-dry clay. We will be hard and brittle toward change. We must remain fluid and willing to change and respond to God's will, whatever that might be. We must become like the greenware clay. There is a great promise in Proverbs that says, "Blessed is the one who fears the LORD always, but whoever hardens his heart will fall into calamity" (Proverbs 28:14).Our hearts must be soft enough to feel, beat, and bleed, showing compassion to those around us. If we become hard-hearted toward sympathy, then we aren't bending to God's will.

If you are feeling closer to bone dry today, do not be afraid. Do you know what happens to bone-dry clay when water is poured on it? It breaks down completely! The clay collapses into a muddy puddle. The clay particles expand with the water, and the clay dust once again becomes soft clay. Remember the chapters about making and mixing clay? Dry clay almost melts when it is doused in water. Let the grace of God flow over you in all of your imperfections. Like the prodigal son, be willing and open to let go of the negativity weighing you down, and let God handle the rest as the Lord of your life.

Jesus tells us, "Whoever believes in me, as the Scripture has said, 'Out of his heart will flow rivers of living water'" (John 7:38). When Christians accept and allow Jesus to change their lives, their hearts soften because of His Living Water. Only through Jesus can we have eternal life. We must accept Him not only as Lord of all creation but also as the Master of our lives. When we submit to God and allow Him to be in control, our dry and brittle hearts will be revived by His eternal life-giving water.

If I put dried-out clay on the wheel, it would crumble and the centripetal force would cause it to fly in all directions. Old, dry clay is not receptive to any change or manipulation except breaking. This example shows us that we must be saturated in God's Word. By reading the Bible, we will make our hearts and minds softer and more receptive to His will, allowing Him to change and center us.

God can take a hard, completely dried out heart and submerge it in the love of Christ. God can allow circumstances to happen for this person to be receptive and open to change. All human beings have dry, brittle hearts until they accept Jesus into their hearts and lives and become Christians. Then, as the believer's baptism symbolizes, their hearts get submerged into the endless Living Water of Christ. Just like the clay, their dry, hard, brittle hearts are reworked and given a new identity. That clay will never be exactly like it was before, just like human beings will never be the same after they become Christians. This is why Paul can write, "Therefore, if anyone is in Christ, he is a new creation. The old has passed away; behold, the new has come" (2 Corinthians 5:17). Paul experienced this complete change himself.

Paul used to be called Saul, a man who hated Christians so much that he hunted and killed them. God met him on the road to Damascus and shone His splendor directly at Saul, who fell down blind. It was only after being completely humbled and visiting Ananias that Saul changed his ways and started following Jesus. God gave him his sight back, and He also softened his heart.

There is always hope for both the leather-hard and bone-dry Christians. God will always forgive and welcome His children home with open arms. We can all be washed with the Living Water and reborn as new Christians with soft hearts, ready to do God's work. All we have to do is ask Him for forgiveness.

We can become dry and barren in our creative lives as well. We can become burned out from overworking ourselves. We can lose inspiration for a number of reasons. We can get caught up in our past failures and fears of future attempts. There are many ways that we can feel dried up artistically. Let me challenge you to pray about these feelings and seek inspiration and energy from the Lord. When we try to get our inspiration from the world, others, and social media, we are not seeking God.

We are warned in Deuteronomy to "Beware lest there be among you a root bearing poisonous and bitter fruit, one who, when he hears the words of this sworn covenant, blesses himself in his heart, saying, 'I shall be safe, though I walk in the stubbornness of my heart.' This will lead to sweeping away of moist and dry alike" (Deuteronomy 29:18–20). We should remain open to change and to new ideas. Our prayer should sound a lot like Psalm 51: "Create in me a clean heart, O God, and renew a right spirit within me" (Psalm 51:10). When God is our inspiration, our imaginations have no limits.

Sometimes our environment can make it difficult to remain inspired by the Spirit of God. The psalmist calls out to God in

Chapter 63, saying, "O God, you are my God; earnestly I seek you; my soul thirsts for you; my flesh faints for you, as in a dry and weary land where there is no water" (Psalm 63:1). He compares his soul deprived of God to a desert land. If this describes you today, know that God hears you.

He sees you, and He has a message for you. Like He told Isaiah, "I will pour water on the thirsty land, and streams on the dry ground; I will pour my Spirit upon your offspring, and my blessing on your descendants" (Isaiah 44:3). If we call out to God, He will save us. James reminds us, "Draw near to God, and he will draw near to you" (James 4:8a). God is willing to have a relationship with us, but we must want it enough to search for Him. God will not hide from us.

Remember that God is all-knowing. He already knows the state of your soul. He knows how drained your spirit feels, and He wants to help give you His strength. All you have to do is ask for renewal through the Living Water of Christ, and God will hear you and bless you.

 *Creativity Challenge:* Find a creative way to hydrate physically and spiritually this week. Make lemonade or herbal tea; maybe have quiet time outdoors or jam out to some praise music.

A kiln firing casualty! This piece was too wet for the kiln and likely had some air bubbles as well. What a mess! That's what I get for rushing things.

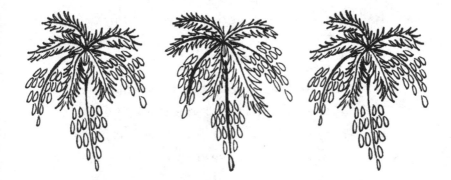

Chapter 11:

Bisque Firing and the Trials of Life

"Now if anyone builds on the foundation with gold, silver, precious stones, wood, hay, straw-each one's work will become manifest, for the Day will disclose it, because it will be revealed by fire, and the fire will test what sort of work each one has done. If the work that anyone has built on the foundation survives, he will receive a reward. If anyone's work is burned up, he will suffer loss, though he himself will be saved, but only as through fire" (1 Corinthians 3:12-15).

"He answered and said, 'But I see four men unbound, walking in the midst of the fire and they are not hurt; and the appearance of the fourth is like a son of the gods'" (Daniel 3:25).

"And the LORD said to Moses and Aaron, 'Take handfuls of soot from the kiln, and let Moses throw them in the air in the sight of Pharaoh. It shall become fine dust over all the land of Egypt, and become boils breaking out in sores on man and beast throughout all the land of Egypt.' So they took soot from the kiln and stood before Pharaoh. And Moses threw it in the air, and it became boils breaking out in sores on man and beast" (Exodus 9:8-10).

"Count it all joy, my brothers, when you meet trials of various kinds, for you know that the testing of your faith produces steadfastness" (James 1:2-3).

"In this you rejoice, though now for a little while, if necessary, you have been grieved by various trials, so that the tested genuineness of your faith—more precious than gold that perishes though it is tested by fire—may be found to result in praise and glory and honor at the revelation of Jesus Christ" (1 Peter 1:6-7).

"Then the Lord knows how to rescue the godly from trials, and to keep the unrighteous under punishment until the day of judgment" (2 Peter 2:9).

"It is the LORD who goes before you. He will be with you; he will not leave you or forsake you. Do not fear or be dismayed" (Deuteronomy 31:8).

"Bear one another's burdens, and so fulfill the law of Christ" (Galatians 6:2).

Most pottery you are familiar with will undergo at least two firings. The first firing, a bisque or biscuit firing, is relatively quick and not very hot in the ceramics world, only reaching around 1,945 degrees Fahrenheit. This first firing turns greenware (finished clay pieces that haven't been fired yet) into bisqueware. It removes all the water and moisture from the piece. A chemical change happens to the clay at this temperature, making the clay bond to itself. The clay is not food safe at the bisque stage because it is still quite porous. The porosity of the clay helps it accept the glaze that will be added in the next chapter.

You can tell the difference between clay that hasn't been fired and the clay that has. If you gently tap on the unfired clay with your fingernail, it will sound dull, like tapping on the granite countertop. If you tap the same way onto bisque-fired pottery, it should give off a high, pinging sound, like a tuning fork. Glazed and vitrified pottery will produce a fuller pinging sound than bisqueware.

The bisque firing is the true test of whether the piece was made correctly. If the vessel had any cracks before firing, the cracks will only get bigger. The piece might warp because it was handled too early in the drying stage or because it did not dry evenly. Sometimes a piece will explode with such force that it causes other pieces in the kiln to break or chip and can even damage the kiln.

Our actions as disciples of Christ can create explosive situations and cracked relationships. We might not realize the impact we have on others' lives. In his letter to the Corinthians, Paul says, "Each one's work will become manifest, for the Day will disclose it, because it will be revealed by fire, and the fire will test what sort of work each one has done" (1 Corinthians 3:13). The heat of the kiln, the fire, reveals the true nature of the piece. The bisque firing solidifies the piece into one solid unit, and the form cannot be easily altered. The similarities in life are amazing; likewise, stressful, tough times reveal our true natures. In the "heat" of the moment, do we stay calm or do we blow up at those around us?

In Daniel 3, three friends literally go inside a fiery furnace. Shadrach, Meshach, and Abednego do not bow down and worship King Nebuchadnezzar's idol, so they are sentenced to die in a kiln most likely used for metals or clay. It is not stated what this furnace was really being used for—perhaps blacksmithing, for making the idol. We do know the kiln was overheated, and it actually burned and killed the men who were sent to throw the three others in.

Nebuchadnezzar then notices four men in the fire; one "is like a son of the gods," and he is walking around unharmed (Daniel 3:25b). Nebuchadnezzar calls the three out of the kiln and blesses their God who saved them from the fire. These men stood amazingly strong under pressure. I love the image of Jesus in the fire with them as well. God proved He is more powerful than earthly trials and softened Nebuchadnezzar's heart in the process. What a testament of faith to face death by fire and still rely on God. The three had no idea what would happen to them. They made no claims about being saved or protected; they only chose to follow God until the end. And just like with the bisqueware, for Shadrach, Meshach, and Abednego, it was not the end!

Like the clay, we change when we undergo hard times. Sometimes, these situations are even referenced symbolically as fire. We, as Christians, have to go through difficult times so that we can mature spiritually. It can be challenging, but this is where it is crucial that we rely on God for our strength and guidance. The clay doesn't know what temperature it needs to be fired to; that is the potter's job to know. We don't know what kinds of trials we need to undergo to become the person God wants us to be, but He does! And the best part is that He also knows how to get us through them as well.

At times like these, it is important to have a good foundation in God and His Word. I love it when a song or Bible verse pops into my head right when I need it. I'll find myself subconsciously humming a tune with no lyrics, but when I focus my attention on the tune, I realize that it is a Christian song with lyrics pertaining to my exact situation!

We all have different levels of trials or fires we must go through. Some seem "hotter" or harder than others. Some people seem to get the "cooler" fires that look like they don't hurt as much as ours. Don't be discouraged! You were made to face the trials specifically designed to make you stronger in *your* faith. *Others* are not created to walk *your* path of life; only you can fulfill God's will for *your* life. You must go through these fires to make yourself and your relationship with God stronger.

Remember Jonah running from God? In Jonah 1, he thought he could escape his fate of going to a foreign area to evangelize, but he ends up just taking the hard way, traveling by whale! But God was with him every step of the journey. God helped Jonah fulfill His will for Jonah's life and for God's plan.

Once Jonah has been swallowed by the whale, he prays to God. We don't always remember this part from the childhood Sunday School lesson. I think this prayer is worth reading:

"Then Jonah prayed to the LORD his God from the belly of the fish, saying, "I called out to the LORD, out of my distress, and he answered me; out of the belly of Sheol I cried, and you heard my voice. For you cast me into the deep, into the heart of the seas, and the flood surrounded me; all your waves and your billows passed over me. Then I said, 'I am driven away from your sight; yet I shall again look upon your holy temple.' The waters closed in over me to take my life; the deep surrounded me; weeds were wrapped around my head at the roots of the mountains. I went down to the land whose bars closed upon me forever; yet you brought up my life from the pit, O LORD my God. When my life was fainting away, I remembered the LORD, and my prayer came to you, into your holy temple. Those who pay regard to vain idols forsake their hope of steadfast love. But I with the voice of thanksgiving will sacrifice to you; what I have vowed I will pay. Salvation belongs to the LORD!" And the LORD spoke to the fish, and it vomited Jonah out upon the dry land" (Jonah 2:1–10).

This is a prayer of both distress and praise. Jonah has recognized and come to accept that God's plan is more important than his life. He prays to God from inside of the fish, asking God for deliverance and promising a sacrifice to God if he makes it out of the fish alive. He could not get out of the fish on his own; he needed God to release him.

In the same way, pots being fired in the kiln cannot get out of the kiln on their own. They can explode inside of the kiln, but they cannot get out of the kiln. The potter cannot remove the pieces from the kiln until the firing is complete (unless this is an alternative firing type). With most firing methods, especially for bisque firings, the pieces must remain in the kiln for the entire firing. If the piece is pulled out of the kiln before it has cooled back off, then the thermal shock could crack the piece.

We must see our trials through to the end. If we are removed from them before the Lord plans, then we might not learn what we are supposed to from the trials. God uses the ashes from most likely a wood kiln to symbolize one of the trials in the Old Testament. God tells Moses and Aaron to "take handfuls of soot from the kiln, and let Moses throw them in the air in the sight of Pharaoh." (Exodus 9:8). The soot became boils on the skin of human beings and animals alike once it had been thrown into the air. This soot is probably wood ash. Wood ash itself can cause skin irritation when mixed with water, but these boils were much worse. These kilns were probably the brick firing kilns the Israelites worked with during their captivity in Egypt.

How appropriate that God would use this symbolism. Slavery and making bricks were trials that the Israelites were facing at that time, especially when Pharaoh kept making it harder and harder to keep up production. These trials were physically and mentally exhausting, and they were killing the Israelites. I'm sure Pharaoh was starting to connect the symbolism, even though God hardened his heart.

Trials aren't just in the Old Testament, though. Many followers of Jesus, especially the disciples, experienced countless trials. James reminds us to "count it all joy, my brothers, when you meet trials of various kinds, for you know that the testing of your faith produces steadfastness" (James 1:2). Facing trials in the name of Jesus can be scary. James says we should be glad that we are strong enough in our faith for others to recognize us as Christians and that God allows us to be put under trials.

Peter says our lives on earth are short, and as Christians we are guaranteed to face trials. He also says, "In this you rejoice, though now for a little while, if necessary, you have been grieved by various trials, so that the tested genuineness of your faith—more precious than gold that perishes though it is tested by fire—may be found to result in praise and glory and honor at the revelation of Jesus Christ" (1 Peter 1:6–8). Peter says that our faith is more valuable than gold and that by keeping our faith even through the heat of the trials, Jesus Christ will be glorified.

Guess what temperature gold melts at? It melts at 1,948 degrees Fahrenheit, but God didn't compare us to gold! We are the clay and He is our Potter! Remember the bisque firing, the first firing, is 1,945 degrees Fahrenheit. The second firing for most clays is the same exact temperature or *even hotter*. Not only is our faith more valuable than gold, but through Christ, it is twice as strong under fire.

Don't worry though; we aren't alone in our faith or in our trials. Peter tells us again, "The Lord knows how to rescue the godly from trials, and to keep the unrighteous under punishment until the day of judgment" (2 Peter 2:9). If God allows us to face trials, then He is right there beside us. He is helping us through our hard times if we ask Him. The potter doesn't forget about the piece in the kiln. The potter can't wait until the firing is over and the kiln is cool enough for the piece to be unloaded. God does not enjoy suffering, and there's no suffering in Heaven.

Unlike the potters here on earth, God can withstand the heat again and again. He is the Potter who is inside the kiln with His clay. He sees everything that happens to them at all times and knows exactly what is going on. He promises us just like He did with Joshua, "It is the LORD who goes before you. He will be with you; he will not leave you or forsake you. Do not fear or be dismayed" (Deuteronomy 31:8). The Lord has already seen what is to come because time cannot constrain Him. He not only walks alongside you, but He has already been there. He guides you every step of the way.

If you asked God to turn down the heat in your trials, you would not be as strong as you are now. You would miss out on the beauty of learning to rely solely on Him. You might crack under the slightest pressure, rendering you useless. I admit that I have not enjoyed my fires. I was resentful about going through back surgery for years. I was mad at the doctor for performing the surgery, and I was also mad at my parents for allowing it to happen. It felt like the surgery had wrecked my entire world. When looking back on it, I can tell it gave me guidance and perseverance. Praying in the months leading up to my surgery brought me closer to God than I had ever thought possible, and now I'm even closer to Him still!

Please seek Christian help if you feel as defeated as I did then. There is nothing wrong with sharing your burdens with others. In fact, it is encouraged: "Bear one another's burdens, and so fulfill the law of Christ" (Galatians 6:2). Paul encourages us to help each other to overcome sins, trials, and struggles, but sometimes, asking for help can be the hardest part. Just like the artist chooses the clay, God chose you specifically to do the purpose He has in mind for you. God is in control. He has chosen the plan for your life. Now, all you have to do is trust in Him!

Creativity Challenge: Learning Bible verses as a child in Sunday School was the foundation I needed to give me strength during difficult times. Even if I don't remember the whole verse, a little snippet running through my head like a mantra can change my mood for the day or the situation. It's never too late to learn verses! Choose a verse that is meaningful to you, write it on a notecard, and place it on a mirror or calendar, somewhere you can look at it every day! Find creative ways to memorize the verse you picked.

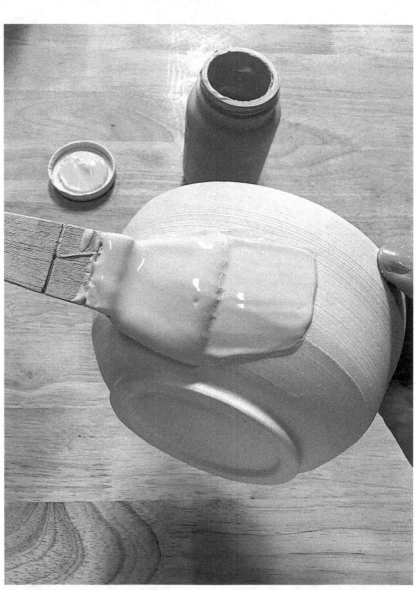

Glazing can feel a lot like painting on a 3D canvas. You can get as detailed as you like. I have to watch where I'm glazing to make sure the pot's foot stays clean. Remember, glaze is glass and will fuse to anything it touches in the kiln, even the kiln itself!

Chapter 12:

Glazing and the Grace of God

"You will say to me then, 'Why does he still find fault? For who can resist his will?' But who are you, O man, to answer back to God? Will what is molded say to its molder, 'Why have you made me like this?' Has the potter no right over the clay, to make out of the same lump one vessel for honorable use and another for dishonorable use?" (Romans 9:19-21).

"Now in a great house there are not only vessels of gold and silver but also of wood and clay, some for honorable use, some for dishonorable. Therefore, if anyone cleanses himself from what is dishonorable, he will be a vessel for honorable use, set apart as holy, useful to the master of the house, ready for every good work" (2 Timothy 2:20-21).

"Then Mordecai told them to reply to Esther, 'Do not think to yourself that in the king's palace you will escape any more than all the other Jews. For if you keep silent at this time, relief and deliverance will rise for the Jews from another place, but you and your father's house will perish. And who knows whether you have not come to the kingdom for such a time as this?'" (Esther 4:13-14).

"Look at the birds of the air: they neither sow nor reap nor gather into barns, and yet your heavenly Father feeds them. Are you not of more value than they? And which of you by being anxious can add a single hour to his span of life? And why are you anxious about clothing? Consider the lilies of the field, how they grow: they neither toil nor spin, yet I tell you, even Solomon in all his glory was not arrayed like one of these. But if God so clothes the grass of the field, which today is alive and tomorrow is thrown into the oven, will he not much more clothe you, O you of little faith?" (Matthew 6:26-30).

"Like the glaze covering an earthen vessel are fervent lips with an evil heart" (Proverbs 26:23).

"When David came to Mahanaim, Shobi the son of Nahash from Rabbah of the Ammonites, and Machir the son of Ammiel from Lo-debar, and Barzillai the Gileadite from Rogelim, brought beds, basins, and earthen vessels, wheat, barley, flour, parched grain, beans, and lentils, honey and curds and sheep and cheese from the herd, for David and the people with him to eat, for they said, 'The people are hungry and weary and thirsty in the wilderness'" (2 Samuel 17:27-29).

"The precious sons of Zion, worth their weight in fine gold, how they are regarded as earthen pots, the work of a potter's hands!" (Lamentations 4:2).

"The one who conquers and who keeps my works until the end, to him I will give authority over the nations, and he will rule them with a rod of iron, as when earthen pots are broken in pieces, even as I myself have received

authority from my Father. And I will give him
the morning star" (Revelation 2:26-28).

I f you've ever painted anything, then you probably know the
final piece won't look exactly like you imagined. When you
start with that blank canvas or white wall, you can feel the
potential. As soon as you slap on that first brushstroke of paint,
it seems like all the potential vanishes. You have picked a color,
and that shows on the surface. It is no longer white; the work
has begun.

The intended use for a clay vessel determines its glaze or
finish. This is true of our spiritual lives as well. It is a hard truth
to learn at times, but God creates each one of us with distinct
strengths and weaknesses. This world will tell us we can be anything we want to be if we just work hard enough, but if God has
not blessed our path, we won't get very far.

Sometimes, on stressful days, I question why God gave me
this desire for pottery. If I'm really physically at a disadvantage
when it comes to pottery, then why am I so drawn to it? God
reminds me and you with a question, "Has the potter no right
over the clay, to make out of the same lump one vessel for honorable use and another for dishonorable use?" (Romans 9:21).
God doesn't make us all rock stars or CEOs of wealthy businesses. A porcelain toilet is not nearly as honorable in my mind
as a porcelain figurine, but it is definitely more needed!

Paul explains, ". . . if anyone cleanses himself from what
is dishonorable, he will be a vessel for honorable use, set apart
as holy, useful to the master of the house, ready for every
good work" (2 Timothy 2:21). We must internally cleanse our

thoughts, hearts, and spirits so that God the Potter can use us for His honorable will.

Glaze can be broken down into the basic elements of clay, water, glass, flux, and, in some cases, pigment. The clay element in the glaze helps it stick to the bisque piece during the glazing process and prevents the glaze from running off the pot in the firing. The water allows the glaze to be applied by brush or by dipping the piece. The glass seals the piece, making it water-proof and durable, and the flux helps to melt the glass. The pig-ment allows the glaze to be colored, giving variety to the work. Glaze can be applied by dipping the piece into it, painting the glaze onto the piece, or spraying it onto the piece in a well-ven-tilated spray booth. Glaze, before it is fired, is pretty toxic, so safety precautions should always be taken.

Before firing, the glaze might not look the color it will turn out when fired. This is the "fun" part. Red and blue do not always make purple in the glaze world. The chemistries in glazes can react to the heat by making different colors or creating some interesting textures, some desired and some . . . not so much. There is little worse than finishing a great pot only to have it ruined by the glaze. The elements and chemicals in the glazes will turn colors when reacting with each other and with the heat of the kiln. Glaze adds strength to the piece, giving it a smooth layer of protection against food and daily use.

There are different types of firings that allow for different techniques. Oxidation firings allow oxygen to circulate contin-uously throughout the kiln and react with the glazes. Reduction firings reduce the oxygen in the kiln toward the end of the firing. This reduced atmosphere is created by blocking off the chimney of the kiln with a damper, cutting off the oxygen from a com-bustible fuel source like wood or gas. Wood ash and soda ash can be added during firings to create different firing atmospheres as well. Raku and pit firings involve smoke and combustible materials. If you've ever seen horsehair pottery, the lines created are the scorch marks of locks of hair that were laid onto the hot piece taken right out of the kiln. Burnt hair creates black lines.

Glazed pieces must be carefully loaded into the kiln because they can stick to each other or to the kiln itself permanently during firing. Since glaze is basically liquid glass, it can run and fuse to almost anything. Every base must be wiped free of glaze before loading the kiln so the pieces will not stick to the shelves during firing.

Depending on how hot the clay is firing, the glaze must be able to withstand that temperature as well. Whichever glaze is chosen, its firing temperature has to match the firing tempera-ture of the clay. If the firing temperatures do not match, then either the clay or glaze will not be fired to the right temperature. Sometimes this leads to under-firing a glaze, causing a chalky texture to form from the glaze instead of a smooth, glassy one. It could also cause over-firing of the glaze, resulting in glaze bubbling and running all over the kiln shelves and ruining the piece. Sometimes the glaze reaches maturity, but the clay is under-fired and porous or over-fired and starts to slump, bloat, or become brittle.

Glaze not only strengthens the piece, but it also serves to beautify it. When we think of beauty in the Bible, one of the women to comes to mind would probably be Esther. The author tells us that she was so beautiful that she was taken into King

Ahasuerus's harem. Her cousin, Mordecai, learned that an official in the king's court, Haman, was planning to destroy all the Jews. Esther rightfully feared death in going against Haman but asked the king for the Jews to be spared. This meant asking the king to go back on his word. It also meant exposing her true identity as a Jew, which she had kept hidden. Last, it meant going to the king even though she wasn't summoned. This alone could have gotten her killed.

She voiced all of her concerns to Mordecai through a servant. Mordecai sent this message back to Esther, "Do not think to yourself that in the king's palace you will escape any more than all the other Jews. For if you keep silent at this time, relief and deliverance will rise for the Jews from another place, but you and your father's house will perish. And who knows whether you have not come to the kingdom for such a time as this?" (Esther 4:13–14). God allowed Esther's beauty to send her into the trial of her life, but He also made it the reason that she was able to spare the Jews.

If she had not been taken by the king in the first place, she would not have had such a close relationship with the king and, therefore, would not have been able to save her people. God gave her the position of queen so she could bring salvation to her people. Her husband spared her and chose to listen to her over Haman because of her strength, wit, grace, and dependence on God.

Jesus says in Matthew, "Look at the birds of the air: they neither sow nor reap nor gather into barns, and yet your heavenly Father feeds them. Are you not of more value than they? And which of you by being anxious can add a single hour to his span of life? And why are you anxious about clothing? Consider the lilies of the field, how they grow: they neither toil nor spin, yet I tell you, even Solomon in all his glory was not arrayed like one of these. But if God so clothes the grass of the field, which today is alive and tomorrow is thrown into the oven, will he not much more clothe you, O you of little faith?" (Matthew 6:2–30).

The pot does not tell the potter what glaze it wants; that's for the potter to decide. We, as Christians, must remember that God's will is most important. We might have plans, but God's will is best. I want to remind us that self-image is not as important as what is inside. Similarly to ceramics, the structure and craftsmanship of the pot are more important than its glaze. A beautifully colored pot with a poor foundation will serve no good purpose. This is so important for every child of God to realize, yet one of the hardest lessons to learn.

Proverbs tells us a similar lesson. The author writes, "Like the glaze covering an earthen vessel are fervent lips with an evil heart" (Proverbs 26:23). The term earthen vessel refers to earthenware clay. This is a lower-firing clay that withholds decently to thermal shock. It is common to find earthenware wild clay in most parts of the world, so this clay would most likely be available.

Glazed pieces would be more expensive and used for special occasions. This verse is saying the piece might look pretty, but it is ordinary on the inside. The fervent lips—or good talk—might sound pleasing, but if that person has an evil heart and does not mean what she says, then there is nothing remarkable about her in the eyes of God.

Earthen vessels are most likely describing daily cookware, water containers, and other utilitarian pots. There are several ref-

erences to earthen vessels that help us decipher what they culturally represent. They appear in record keeping:

> "When David came to Mahanaim, Shobi the
> son of Nahash from Rabbah of the Ammo-
> nites, and Machir the son of Ammiel from
> Lo-debar, and Barzillai the Gileadite from
> Rogelim, brought beds, basins, and earthen
> vessels, wheat, barley, flour, parched grain,
> beans, and lentils, honey and curds and
> sheep and cheese from the herd, for David
> and the people with him to eat, for they
> said, "The people are hungry and weary and
> thirsty in the wilderness" (2 Samuel 17:27-29).

These earthen pots must have been useful in the wilderness
because they were mentioned as their own unit. They weren't
described as full of a more valuable item, although they probably were used for storage. They might have held water to
keep it clean. These earthen vessels were the essentials, not
the prized heirlooms. In Lamentations, we get another reference. The author says, "The precious sons of Zion, worth
their weight in fine gold, how they are regarded as earthen
pots, the work of a potter's hands!" (Lamentations 4:2). Once
again, the earthen vessels represent the unexciting. The book

of Lamentations retells the destruction that has befallen Zion. This verse is saying that even sons, those who should culturally be prized in a family because they will inherit and provide for the family's name and legacy, are treated as everyday earthen pots. They are overlooked because of all the turmoil and hopelessness.

In Revelation, we get yet another reference. Jesus says through John's visions, "The one who conquers and who keeps my works until the end, to him I will give authority over the nations, and he will rule them with a rod of iron, as when earthen pots are broken in pieces, even as I myself have received authority from my Father" (Revelation 2:26–27). Those who have been faithful to Jesus and His commands will be allowed to have authority. Instead of Nebuchadnezzar's dream of everything being crushed by stone, now Christ's followers will use iron to break apart nations as easily as breaking earthen vessels.

I'm sure you've seen one of those red-orange terra cotta flower pots that taper and feel rough to the touch. That is a good example of an earthen vessel. It, in fact, is made of earthenware clay. It is just an everyday pot, easily overlooked. It would be easy to smash it with an iron rod. If you put some glaze on it, it might be prettier to look at, but it is still the same red-orange clay underneath. God does not compare His children to these pots in this reference. No, we are special to Him. We are worth celebrating over when we return to Him because He cares deeply for us, His creation.

The matching and melding of clay and glaze allow for vitrification. Vitrification occurs when the clay has been fired to the beginning of its melting temperature. All the clay particles will melt and seal together at this stage, making the piece waterproof. If you fire too much hotter than this, your clay will melt. Earthenware clay fires at such a low temperature because the iron in the clay melts at lower temperatures. The iron is what gives the clay that red-orange color.

The clay has not been fully fired to its mature temperature until the glaze firing. The bisque firing only begins with what the glaze firing completes, similar to how Adam only began what Jesus completed. Adam and Eve sinned, but they could not pay the price for their sins. Jesus came to be the human sacrifice to pay for the sins of humanity. Jesus finished and corrected what Adam and Eve had ruined: a sinless and personal relationship with God. Just like a glazed piece appears more brilliant than a bisque piece, Jesus's death, resurrection, and ascension produced a brilliant salvation for humanity, but it is not the conclusion! Jesus is coming back for us!

Glaze is similar to the Holy Spirit entering into a new Christian's life. We can't help but spread Jesus's love and share our testimony. We look different, too; we are smiling, radiant and glowing. Like the glaze is fused to the pot, Christians are completely sealed by God and covered in the sacrifice that Jesus made for us. Yes, we are still sinful, but Jesus's sacrifice, grace, and forgiveness coat our lives in the eyes of the Lord, allowing us to have personal relationships with Him. Just like fired glaze cannot be removed from a pot, nothing can separate us from God's love. This isn't to say we won't face struggles, injury, or illness. God still allows those trials of life, but once we ask Jesus to transform our lives, we will never be alone again. God's grace covers us.

Within the variety of glazes, each one holds a different purpose. Just like the glazes, everyone is created for a purpose. Just because someone else has different talents from us, it does not make either of us more important. God has given all of us unique skill sets for a specific reason, to fulfill His purpose in our lives.

Creativity Challenge: Create a self-portrait. What do you see superficially, just from looking at the picture? Now cover the picture in affirmations and verses of who God says you are. What has God told you is His plan for you? How can that interior reflect onto your exterior self?

PART 3

Honoring God Creatively

My kiln is top loading, so this angle is taken from the top looking down into the kiln during a kiln loading session. I've still got some more room for adding more shelves and pots to the load before firing.

Chapter 13:

Opening the Kiln: Christmas or Rapture?

"Be sober-minded; be watchful. Your adversary the devil prowls around like a roaring lion, seeking someone to devour" (1 Peter 5:8).

"Now Mount Sinai was wrapped in smoke because the LORD had descended on it in fire. The smoke of it went up like the smoke of a kiln, and the whole mountain trembled greatly" (Exodus 19:18).

"And these will go away into eternal pun-ishment, but the righteous into eternal life" (Matthew 25:46).

"These were the potters who were inhabitants of Netaim and Gederah. They lived there in the king's service" (1 Chronicles 4:23).

"When the Son of Man comes in his glory, and all the angels with him, then he will sit on his glorious throne. Before him will be gathered all the nations, and he will sep-arate people one from another as a shep-herd separates the sheep from the goats" (Matthew 25:31-32).

"You shall therefore separate the clean beast from the unclean, and the unclean bird from the clean. You shall not make yourselves detestable by beast or by bird or by anything with which the ground crawls, which I have set apart for you to hold unclean. You shall be holy to me, for I the LORD am holy and have separated you from the peoples, that you should be mine" (Leviticus 20:25-26).

"And Ezra the priest stood up and said to them, 'You have broken faith and married foreign women, and so increased the guilt of Israel. Now then make confession to the LORD, the God of your fathers and do his will. Separate yourselves from the peoples of the land and from the foreign wives'" (Ezra 10:10-11).

"And the Israelites separated themselves from all foreigners and stood and confessed their sins and the iniquities of their fathers" (Nehemiah 9:2).

"Separate yourselves from among this congregation, that I may consume them in a moment" (Numbers 16:21).

". . . and its breaking is like that of a potter's vessel that is smashed so ruthlessly that among its fragments not a shard is found with which to take fire from the hearth or to dip up water out of the cistern" (Isaiah 30:14).

"But we have this treasure in jars of clay, to show that the surpassing power belongs to God and not to us" (2 Corinthians 4:7).

"You shall break them with a rod of iron and dash them in pieces like a potter's vessel" (Psalm 2:9).

Many ceramic artists compare opening the glaze kiln to the excitement of Christmas morning. I think that this is a great analogy, although I don't always agree. Waiting to open a kiln can be exciting and nerve-wracking. The anticipation of waiting to see the results reminds me of waiting for Christmas morning. The results, however, aren't always akin to unwrapping Christmas presents. I've never received broken art as a Christmas gift, but I have gotten that experience from a kiln opening.

I experienced a series of bad firings after I started to use my first kiln. During two different firings, shelves cracked, resulting in pieces getting destroyed. During another firing, a shelf completely split in half, ruining the pieces it fell on top of as well as the pieces it was holding, which all slid together. Of course, this kiln load housed a custom order I had been working on, and I was going to film the kiln opening live on social media. We know from glazing that when the glaze touches something in the kiln, it fuses to it. Four of the cups fused together during that firing, along with some other odd craziness: pieces warping or having bits of shelf stuck to them. Thankfully, I've never had a Christmas that bad.

When the original Christmas began on Earth, God broke the silence that had lasted four hundred years. His people were waiting with anticipation for a coming Savior. What joy descended on the world when Jesus came! Some of that joy is reflected each Christmas morning when children rush downstairs to open gifts, which "Santa," family, and friends have given them. We want to show how much we love each other by giving gifts we think others will like. God showed us His love for humanity by sending His only Son to be sacrificed so we could have a relationship with Him, be forgiven of our sins, and live eternally with Him.

As for the kiln firings, the artist has been waiting for this moment for a long time. She has completed all the steps to create a finished piece. She has learned how to adjust her techniques and glazes to get the look she is going for. She has remade broken, imperfect, and cracked work in order to reach her desired level of craftsmanship. Now it is time to see if all of her hard work has paid off. When the kiln is opened, and the artist can see her handiwork, it is one of the greatest feelings of accomplishment! She feels relief that the pieces are safe and also takes pride in her accomplishments.

Wait, What Is a Kiln?

I realize probably not everyone knows what a kiln is. A kiln is made of bricks and contains pots and hot temperatures. The materials that go into making a kiln share characteristics with volcanic materials. There are several types of kilns depending on location, culture, firing techniques, and materials.

The simplest way to fire pottery is a technique called "pit firing." Essentially, you dig a hole in the ground. The hole must be deep but shallow enough to prevent any flammable debris from causing the fire to spread. Digging into a patch of clay works well.

Then you line the pit you have dug with flammable things like wood, grass and leaves. You place your pieces inside and then cover them with more brush. Next, you light the whole thing on fire, and there you have it! Once the fire dies down, you'll be able to take out your pots. This method isn't ideal anymore because it is hard to judge the heat of the firing and difficult to do with food-safe glazed wares.

Gas, soda, wood, and salt kilns can all produce reduction firings. This means that through opening and closing the ventilation systems at different times in the firing process, you can reduce and restrict the amount of oxygen entering the kiln. This will make the glaze appear differently. It can affect the color and texture of glazes, and special reduction glazes have been created to use with these gas firings. Propane and natural gas can both be used to fire kilns. Gas kilns can be built of brick like the others, or they can resemble train cars, and the kiln can be loaded and unloaded with carts on wheels and tracks.

There are, of course, many alternative firing processes. These include, but are not limited to, raku firing, saggar firing, microwave kilns, top hat kilns, and sawdust firings.

Wood kilns are like long tunnels made of bricks. They can also be built into a hill or an embankment to help with the structure. They have a chimney to promote airflow and ventilation. If you are familiar with Chinese pottery culture, Dragon and Anagama climbing kilns fall into this category. They can be big enough around that a person could crawl through or walk through for loading and unloading. There would be a designated space for the burning wood and holes in the walls with brick plugs to be used like corks or stoppers for inserting more wood during the firing and blocking the air from escaping when wood is not being added.

Soda kilns can also be large enough for a person to enter. They are made of brick and can be wood- or gas-powered. A mixture of soda ash or sodium carbonate is dissolved in water and is sprayed inside the kiln to add to the atmosphere during the firing. This will create different results on the surfaces of the pots. This is similar to salt firings, where the artists introduce salt into the kiln's atmosphere, but the salt is not dissolved in water.

Beehive kilns and bottle kilns are industrial kilns with a little more controlled firing atmosphere. A beehive kiln is a European style of kiln that looks like old-fashioned man-made bee beehives. Bottle kilns look very similar in structure, like a glass bottle. Ceramics factories used these kilns for production, but both have fallen out of popularity.

Electric kilns are most common in classroom settings and home studios, and they rarely produce reduction results. These kilns run off of electricity and depending on your wiring, they can plug in or be wired into your home's electrical box. Electric kilns are built with a lighter and more porous, soft brick as opposed to the more cement-like, hard firebrick used to build the wood and gas kilns. Electric kilns produce an oxidation firing atmosphere. They have fans to constantly pull the toxins, which the glaze and clay emit, from the firing atmosphere and deposit the fumes safely out of the area in which you are firing. Glazes in oxidation firings tend to be brighter because oxygen is not reduced at any point during the firing. They can also be brighter because electric kilns typically fire at lower temperatures than gas, wood, salt, and soda kilns, although some can reach the hotter temperatures as well. The hotter the firing, the more of a chance for the colors to "burn out" and become dull. Electric kilns have a protective metal sleeve around them to keep all the bricks in place and tend to stand off of the ground on a stilted stand. They can be top loading or front loading and come in all different shapes and sizes.

Sometimes, depending on how the kiln fires, there can still be some mishaps and disappointments: the glaze runs, the glaze turns the wrong shade, the piece warps because of the heat of the firing, the piece cracks, the glaze pinholes, or the glaze crawls, shivers, bloats, etc. Sometimes the piece does not come out as planned. This is because, in this world, imperfection is inevitable. We live in a fallen world where "the devil prowls around like a roaring lion, seeking someone to devour" (1 Peter 5:8). We can't fix all the problems in the world. All we can do is learn from our mistakes and try again, which is what God asks of us.

If a clay body is fired at a temperature that is too hot, the iron and other materials in the clay could cause it to melt. If a clay is fired at a temperature that is too low, it will not be properly vitrified and will be more apt to crack, break, or leak. As we learned in previous chapters, vitrification occurs when the clay's chemical compounds are melted together properly to form a strong bond. When a piece is vitrified, all the particles in the clay and glaze have reached their optimal melting points for the desired results. They have formed a bond so strong that the piece becomes water tight. As long as the glaze does not have toxic materials, then it has the potential to be food safe after firing.

I imagine the final judgment day, when Jesus returns to earth, to be a little like opening a kiln. After all, the Old Testament talks what it was like when God came down to Mount Sinai: "The smoke of it went up like the smoke of a kiln" (Exodus 19:18a). The mountain smoked because of the fire of the Lord.

One of the alternative firing methods I mentioned is called "raku." Our westernized version of raku looks a lot different from how it began. If you are familiar with horsehair pottery, then you've seen raku ware. In this firing method, the glowing red pieces are taken out of the kiln with long metal tongs and thrown directly into a metal container or pit filled with combustible materials like paper, wood, feathers, and hair. The piece is so hot that it immediately sets these items on fire—no spark needed. I imagine God's entrance in Exodus to be like that, pure power.

Not every piece that comes out of the kiln is pleasing to the potter. There are often disappointments. Similarly, Matthew relays Jesus's account of the coming judgment. Jesus explains that when He returns, ". . . he will separate people one from another as a shepherd separates the sheep from the goats" (Matthew 25:31–32). He will divide those who love and serve Him from those who don't.

Again, the artist separates the spoiled work from her best work. The best work will be used in art shows, exhibitions, and fairs or sold. In the case of the Old Testament, the king could have several "potters who . . . lived there in the king's service" (1 Chronicles 4:23). What an honor but also a very stressful job! Their best work would go to the king. It would be placed high in honor, a focal point for all to see.

The ruined work, if it is beyond use (not food safe, dangerously sharp, cracked, etc.) is thrown away. This work is not even useful for sales. It has no value and must be discarded to make more room for new work. Some potters choose to break their unworthy pots rather than let them get into the public's hands. Studios can have what is called "a boneyard"—a designated place to get rid of pottery that isn't good enough to sell. Potters will throw the unworthy pots onto the bone pile, a mound full of other broken and unworthy pots.

God separates His children, those who follow Him, from the people who choose not to accept Him as their Lord and Savior. In the final verse of the passage in Matthew 25, Jesus says, "And these will go away into eternal punishment, but the righteous into eternal life" (Matthew 25:46). On Judgment Day, those who follow Christ will be separated from those who don't.

In the Old Testament, God tells His people again and again to remove themselves from bad influences. He reminds them they are His people, saying, "You shall be holy to me, for I the LORD am holy and have separated you from the peoples, that you should be mine" (Leviticus 20:26). He has set His people apart. To follow God, they must remember who they are in the eyes of the Lord and separate themselves from evil.

Another Old Testament prophet, Ezra, receives a similar message from God that he must share with the people. Ezra tells them, "You have broken faith and married foreign women, and so increased the guilt of Israel. Now then make confession to the LORD, the God of your fathers and do his will. Separate yourselves from the peoples of the land and from the foreign wives" (Ezra 10:10–11). The people listened and turned away from their sins.

Their hearts were softened and opened enough to listen to the words of God spoken through the prophets. In another scenario, "The Israelites separated themselves from all foreigners and stood and confessed their sins and the iniquities of their fathers" (Nehemiah 9:2). They understand what happens to those who refuse to follow God. They don't want to end up like the pots in the bone pile.

In Numbers, we have another separating situation. Korah, who was part of the tribe of Levi, gathers men together and rebels against Moses and Aaron. He is jealous of how holy and set apart Moses and Aaron seem to be. He doesn't understand or want to believe that God chose to set these two men apart. God is displeased with the revolt and tells Moses and Aaron that He will destroy the entire gang, saying, "Separate yourselves from among this congregation, that I may consume them in a moment" (Numbers 16:21). Moses and Aaron beg for the lives of the followers of Korah because they weren't in charge. God allows the entire congregation to be spared. God uses a sink hole to swallow up Korah and the other responsible leaders. He separates the bad influences from His people to protect them.

God, in His might, can use His power to save us when we ask for it or, sometimes, if others ask on our behalf. We, on the other hand, are fragile compared to God's majesty. Sickness, injury, and daily stress remind us that we are only human. God, through Isaiah, warns that the people of Judah wrongly rely on Egypt, which will cause destruction so bad that it can be compared to a "potter's vessel that is smashed so ruthlessly that among its fragments not a shard is found with which to take fire from the hearth or to dip up water out of the cistern" (Isaiah 30:14b). But don't worry, God still loves His people, even in their mistakes. He uses the hard and painful consequences we experience to draw us back into His will.

God can be glorified because of our frailty. Yes, we are physically weak, but the Holy Spirit inside of us is strong; "We have this treasure in jars of clay, to show that the surpassing power belongs to God and not to us" (2 Corinthians 4:7). We praise God who delivers us from our own inadequacies. The treasure of the Gospel and the Holy Spirit in us as Christians is even more powerful than our human bodies. The Lord will conquer all evil. He promises victory over foreign nations to the Psalmist, saying, "You shall break them with a rod of iron and dash them in pieces like a potter's vessel" (Psalm 2:9). This time, broken pottery reveals the victory that God will grant us if we ask Him.

Creativity Challenge: Have you ever waited for something with severe anticipation? Create something that can't be finished in one sitting. Bake cookies without eating one until the next day. Sit there and watch your paint dry. Photograph using long exposure. Now, reflect on how you felt during the waiting and during the results as well.

These three wheel-thrown pots are my example of marbled clay. I mixed
three differently colored clays together by wedging and then throwing
them on the wheel to create this swirled, marbled look. If I kept wedging, I
could blend the clays completely to make one solid color.

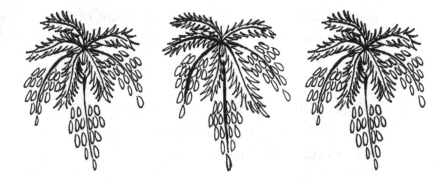

Chapter 14:

The Potter's House on Earth and in Heaven

"Your maxims are proverbs of ashes; your defenses are defenses of clay" (Job 13:12).

"Draw water for the siege; strengthen your forts; go into the clay; tread the mortar; take hold of the brick mold!" (Nahum 3:14).

"Now the pots, the shovels, and the basins, all these vessels in the house of the LORD, which Hiram made for King Solomon, were burnished bronze. In the plain of the Jordan the king cast them, in the clay ground between Succoth and Zarethan" (1 Kings 7:45-46).

"In the plain of the Jordan the king cast them, in the clay ground between Succoth and Zeredah" (2 Chronicles 4:17).

"So they took counsel and bought with them the potter's field as a burial place for strangers. Therefore that field has been called the Field of Blood to this day. Then was fulfilled what had been spoken by the prophet Jeremiah, saying, 'And they took the thirty pieces of silver, the price of him on whom a price had been set by some of the sons of Israel, and they gave them for the potter's field, as the Lord directed me'" (Matthew 27:7-10).

"Then I said to them, 'If it seems good to you, give me my wages; but if not, keep them.' And they weighed out as my wages thirty pieces of silver. Then the LORD said to me, 'Throw it to the potter'—the lordly price at which I was priced by them. So I took the thirty pieces of silver and threw them into the house of the LORD, to the potter. Then I broke my second staff Union, annulling

the brotherhood between Judah and Israel"
(Zechariah 11:12-14).

"I am the good shepherd. The good shepherd lays down his life for the sheep"
(John 10:11).

"So I went down to the potter's house, and
there he was working at his wheel. And the
vessel he was making of clay was spoiled in
the potter's hand, and he reworked it into
another vessel, as it seemed good to the
potter to do. Then the word of the LORD
came to me: 'O house of Israel, can I not do
with you as this potter has done?' declares
the LORD. 'Behold, like the clay in the potter's hand, so are you in my hand, O house
of Israel'" (Jeremiah 18:3-6).

"And we know that for those who love God
all things work together for good, for those
who are called according to his purpose"
(Romans 8:28).

"Thus says the LORD, 'Go, buy a potter's
earthenware flask, and take some of the elders
of the people and some of the elders of the
priests, and go out to the Valley of the Son
of Hinnom at the entry of the Potsherd Gate,

and proclaim there the words that I tell you. You shall say, "Hear the word of the LORD, O kings of Judah and inhabitants of Jerusalem. Thus says the LORD of hosts, the God of Israel: Behold, I am bringing such disaster upon this place that the ears of everyone who hears of it will tingle . . ." (Jeremiah 19:1-3).

"The wall was built of jasper, while the city was pure gold, like clear glass. The foundations of the wall of the city were adorned with every kind of jewel. The first was jasper, the second sapphire, the third agate, the fourth emerald, the fifth onyx, the sixth carnelian, the seventh chrysolite, the eighth beryl, the ninth topaz, the tenth chrysoprase, the eleventh jacinth, the twelfth amethyst. And the twelve gates were twelve pearls, each of the gates made of a single pearl, and the street of the city was pure gold, like transparent glass. And I saw no temple in the city, for its temple is the Lord God the Almighty and the Lamb" (Revelation 21:18-22).

Finally, we arrive at the potter's house. I'm sure Jeremiah 18 is most likely what came to mind when you considered what a book about God and pottery could be about. Well, I've got to be honest with you; I've been saving it. If we had jumped right into Jeremiah 18, I was afraid you wouldn't have the technical background you have now. This story is so much more amazing when we come to it knowing more about pottery. Aren't you glad we waited? Now that we have walked through the processes and techniques of pottery, let's consider what Jeremiah's first audience would have known about clay.

As you now know, clay was very important in biblical culture, and honestly, it still has significance in most cultures today. We see this through historical context found in other verses. Job, chronologically one of the oldest books of the Bible, shows a man who never blames God, even amid great suffering. His friends try to comfort him, but honestly, they just cause him more grief. Job tells his friends, "Your maxims are proverbs of ashes; your defenses are defenses of clay" (Job 13:12). He's saying their words are nothing compared to God's strength, and they provide little comfort. Their arguments against God over Job's suffering are like crumbling clay compared to God's majesty.

We get another reference in Nahum. Nahum the Prophet foretells the destruction of Nineveh, which was "the arrogant capital of the Assyrian Empire." Nahum says to Nineveh, "Draw water for the siege; strengthen your forts; go into the clay; tread the mortar; take hold of the brick mold!" (Nahum 3:14). He knows it will all be useless because he believes in the power of his God; he taunts his oppressors, knowing that the city will fall. The clay in reference to the brick mold most likely is describing a brick-making area of the town. Nahum is implying that even if the people make more bricks to add a wall of protection, Nineveh will fall and Judah, God's people, will be rescued.

We also get a reference to the clay ground in 1 Kings and again in 2 Chronicles. The account reads, "In the plain of the Jordan the king cast them, in the clay ground between Succoth and Zeredah" (2 Chronicles 4:17). The clay in the ground proved useful in the process of casting bronze. These verses show the area was good for clay, and that clay wasn't just used for making pots. You could use it to cast bronze and make clay bricks as well.

In the New Testament, we once again get a reference to clay in the ground. After Judas betrays Jesus for thirty pieces of silver, he returns the money to the priests. The church officials didn't know what to do with that sinful money, "So they took counsel and bought with them the potter's field as a burial place for strangers." Therefore, that field has been called the Field of Blood to this day. Then was fulfilled what had been spoken by the prophet Jeremiah, saying, "And they took the thirty pieces of silver, the price of him on whom a price had been set by some of the sons of Israel, and they gave them for the potter's field, as the Lord directed me" (Matthew 27:7–10). The Potter's field would have been a field where clay was easily accessible. The potter would go out and dig clay from it, leaving holes in the field. This was probably a quick way for burying strangers because the holes were already dug.

This verse references Jeremiah, the Old Testament prophet, because of all the verses pertaining to clay and the potter's house. It also is referencing Zechariah. After the prophet Zechariah had become a shepherd, as God had asked him to, the people paid him for his work. Then Zechariah recounts how God told him to take the payment and, "'Throw it to the potter'—the lordly price at which I was priced by them, So I took the thirty pieces of silver and threw them into the house of the LORD, to the potter" (Zechariah 11:1–14). I believe that this verse is directly related to the events in Matthew.

The thirty pieces of silver given to the potter foreshadow the priests using the same amount to purchase the potter's land. God is revealing that the priests who paid Judas to betray Jesus and then used the same money to buy the potter's field are just like the shepherd that God commanded Zechariah to become. Jesus tells us that He is "the good shepherd. The good shepherd lays down his life for the sheep" (John 10:11). The priests were foolish shepherds because they led their flocks astray. I love this connection; our Good Shepherd will never foolishly betray or abandon us. He will be with us through the Holy Spirit as we are on earth, and we will see Him in Heaven.

With every task we set out to accomplish, there are trials, risks, mistakes to be made, and hardships to be had. Ceramics is no different; in fact, it seems to be a mistake enhancer. There are countless ways to ruin a nice piece of art before it is completed. Air bubbles and moisture can do some damage, but they're not the only ones. Another method of unintentional destruction is drying times. If the clay dries too quickly, it can crack. This especially affects handles and the bases of thrown forms. If the clay is too wet, it might sag or collapse on the wheel. Wet clay will be too sticky for hand-building. Sticky clay leaves a poor texture on the forms and is just simply hard to work with. It gets stuck on one's hands, making it nearly impossible to mold. Dry clay is a beast of its own on the wheel. It becomes obstinate and will hardly budge. If the clay dries unevenly, it is prone to all kinds of problems including warping, cracking, and bloating.

If the clay is fired while it is still wet, it will most likely crack or explode. If the clay is fired at the wrong temperature, it will either be under-fired or over-fired. The temperature a clay can take depends on the different types of clays mentioned earlier. If the clay is under-fired, meaning it did not get as hot as it is supposed to, then the clay is not vitrified. It might not hold water, is most likely not food safe, and is brittle, prone to breaking easily. If the clay is over-fired, then the chemical elements in the clay body have begun to melt, not being able to withstand the hot temperatures. At the least, the clay might warp, bloat, sag, or slump; at the worst, the clay will melt down the shelves of the kiln, reminiscent of Salvador Dali's clocks.

In the kiln, pieces can crack, crumble, and collapse. They can warp, slump, bloat, and explode. Handles can crack in half or fall off completely. Wet clay will explode in the kiln. Thick clay will crack or explode. Thin clay will warp or break. To and from the kiln, pieces can be dropped, bumped, or chipped. The glaze can crawl, craze, run, drip, blush, pinhole, shiver, and discolor. Glaze can run and stick to the shelves, meaning the piece is also stuck to the shelves and must be chiseled off. The kiln itself can misfire.

Kilns are like cars; they need constant maintenance. Sometimes elements and parts in a kiln will go bad mid-firing, causing disasters inside. There is a never-ending list of reasons for pieces getting messing up. The artist must trust in her craftsmanship when making work. When outside forces negatively affect the pieces, the potter must see if anything can be improved in the process and then start over. Some problems, like the ones caused by humidity and weather, are beyond anyone's control.

Once I had thrown a large decorative bowl. I had wedged two different colored clays together with the desire to create a unique piece. The two clays responded differently when thrown, and despite my frustration, I proceeded with the piece, even though I had not completely centered it. I couldn't get the handle of centering clay that was half-soft and half-gritty. In the end, I had one very off-centered "bowl-thing." I put it in the sun to dry and tried to trim it the very same day, another mistake on my part. Thrown greenware is so wet from throwing that it usually needs a day (or several) to set up before trimming.

Well, of course, the clay was too wet to trim. And, because of my clay mixing, I discovered a lot more air bubbles than I even thought I had. I kept trying to trim the piece thinner to remove the air bubbles. The clay kept sliding and bending under its own weight because it was so wet and now thin. Eventually, the clay had had enough and flew off of the wheel, marred and mangled, onto the floor. I completely lost that piece because I was impatient. I couldn't have learned that lesson any other way, even though it felt devastating to lose the piece. Thankfully, God always has His perfect timing.

Unfortunately, I, like many other ceramic artists, have experienced many of these kiln problems. They can be heartbreaking and can affect the artist's mental state. I was so frustrated with myself and the clay. I started wondering if a degree in ceramics was the right path for me. I didn't know what to do to fix my problems. It seemed no matter how hard I worked, the clay could "sense" my fear and crack under pressure. It is hard to go back to working when you have had a major disappointment. You doubt yourself, your abilities, and your purpose. Thankfully, because of God's grace, we can ask Him to guide us in His will and purpose for our lives.

Jeremiah witnessed this visual depiction and symbolic meaning firsthand. God instructs Jeremiah to go visit the village potter. While he is there, he sees the potter throwing vessels on the wheel. The vessel is messed up and destroyed. We don't know why it was messed up. Maybe the clay was too wet. It could have been a number of things, but based on the rest of the story, I like to think that it was off-centered. Either way, the vessel falls to the wheel head. The potter takes the clay and reforms it into a new vessel, "as it seemed good to the potter to do" (Jeremiah 18:4b). I'm assuming he lets it dry out a little and gives it a good wedge to mix it, but again, we don't know, and that's not the focal point of the story.

God shows Jeremiah that although Israel has messed up, God still holds them in His hand. Sometimes we must become broken to allow Jesus to make us whole. Just as the clay had to be reworked, the journey will be challenging. God is still giving them—and us—another chance!

God must allow us to suffer sometimes in this life. If He saved us from pain and suffering every time, then we wouldn't rely on Him. In fact, we wouldn't even think we need Him because our lives would always be perfect. It's kind of like that saying, how would we know what justice, happiness, and fairness look like without also seeing injustice, unhappiness, and unfairness? We live in a fallen world.

What Jeremiah does not see is the preparation and practice that went into the potter making that one pot. We don't always see what God is working on behind the scenes that will help us in the future. I do know this, "For those who love God all things work together for good, for those who are called according to his purpose" (Romans 8:28). If we are aligned with God's good will, then we have no need to worry.

The Master Potter

I love to envision God as the Master Potter. Even though we mess up, He tells us He is not giving up on us. He will get us back on the wheel and recenter us. This grace is beautiful. God continues to use clay symbolism to warn His people. In Jeremiah, Chapter 19, God, through Jeremiah, warns His people through the visual of broken pottery that He is "bringing such disaster upon this place that the ears of everyone who hears of it will tingle" (3b). Change and redemption are not always painless. Sometimes, God must allow our hearts to get broken before we are ready to accept His restoration.

It hit me one day that there will be some form of creativity in Heaven because of God's creative nature. This new realization excited me so much. If there is no pain and crying in Heaven and everything is perfect, then there are no mistakes or off-centered clay! How much more enjoyable will creativity be when we know everything will be made for the Lord?

John's visions in Revelation give us a small glimpse of what eternity will be like. In describing the New Heaven and New Earth, he says, "The wall was built of jasper, while the city was pure gold, like clear glass" (Revelation 21:18). By now, we should all know the One who designed this beauty. If we thought God's imagination and creativity for Earth were astounding, just wait until God creates the New Heaven and New Earth! We won't need the sun's light because God's glory will be the brightness, and the darkness of night won't exist. The New Heaven and New Earth won't have churches to worship and praise God in because "its temple is the Lord God the Almighty and the Lamb" (Revelation 21:23). God is fully sufficient; all of the New Heaven and New Earth will be a place to worship God. The purity and loveliness are more beautiful than we can even imagine, and everything will point all the glory and praise back to God. Wow! What a wonderful thing to look forward to, but in the meantime, let us share a glimpse of Heaven with those around us through our creative abilities from God.

Creativity Challenge: The best challenge I can leave you with is to create Heaven on earth for non-believers. Show them God's love and forgiveness through your actions, words, and art! Pray for their hearts to become as soft as fresh clay and that they will be receptive to the Living Water.

This little cream pitcher I made now has a second life
after I put it back together using the ancient kintsugi technique.

Chapter 15:

Go Forth and Remember Your Creator

Conclusion

"Can mortal man be in the right before God? Can a man be pure before his Maker? Even in his servants he puts no trust, and his angels he charges with error; how much more those who dwell in houses of clay, whose foundation is in the dust, who are crushed like the moth" (Job 4:17-19).

"Though he heap up silver like dust, and pile up clothing like clay, he may pile it up, but the righteous will wear it, and the innocent will divide the silver" (Job 27:16-17).

"And he said, 'Naked I came from my mother's womb, and naked shall I return. The LORD gave, and the LORD has taken away; blessed be the name of the LORD'" (Job 1:21).

"Being then God's offspring, we ought not to think that the divine being is like gold or silver or stone, an image formed by the art and imagination of man. The times of ignorance God overlooked, but now he commands all people everywhere to repent, because he has fixed a day on which he will judge the world in righteousness by a man whom he has appointed; and of this he has given assurance to all by raising him from the dead" (Acts 17:29-31).

"Now may the God of peace who brought again from the dead our Lord Jesus, the great shepherd of the sheep, by the blood of the eternal covenant, equip you with everything good that you may do his will, working in us that which is pleasing in his sight, through Jesus Christ, to whom be the glory forever and ever. Amen" (Hebrews 13:20-21).

"It is the LORD who goes before you. He will be with you; he will not leave you or forsake you. Do not fear or be dismayed" (Deuteronomy 31:8).

"And the LORD went before them by day in a pillar of cloud to lead them along the way, and by night in a pillar of fire to give them light, that they might travel by day and by night. The pillar of cloud by day and the pillar of fire by night did not depart from before the people" (Exodus 13:21-22).

"And he opened his mouth and taught them, saying: Blessed are the poor in spirit, for theirs is the kingdom of heaven, Blessed are those who mourn, for they shall be comforted. Blessed are the meek, for they shall inherit the earth. Blessed are those who hunger and thirst for righteousness, for they shall be satisfied. Blessed are the merciful, for they shall receive mercy. Blessed are the pure in heart, for they shall see God. Blessed are the peacemakers, for they shall be called sons of God. Blessed are those who are persecuted for righteousness' sake, for theirs is the kingdom of heaven. Blessed are you when others revile you and persecute you and utter all kinds of evil against you falsely on my account. Rejoice and be glad, for your reward is great in heaven" (Matthew 5:2-12).

We are quickly approaching the end of this book, but don't let your creativity end with the words I've written! We have been on quite a journey, and it would be a shame to stop here. We have identified what creativity is and where it came from. We have acknowledged that our perfectly creative God has given us all the ability to be creative. We have seen how God made pottery beautifully symbolic to His relationship with us. We have studied Jeremiah 18, the most elaborate passage on clay in the Bible. Now we are coming out on the other side of our study.

I want to challenge you to use your wonderful creativity to honor God. That doesn't mean that all you're allowed to paint is Bible verses. Far from it! I'm more trying to warn you against letting your creativity become an idol in your life. Remember Who gave you this gift.

Heading back into the book of Job, we read a response from Eliphaz who clearly didn't have his theology exactly right. He tells Job that God allows his afflictions as punishments for some sin Job must have committed. He asks Job, "Can mortal man be in the right before God? Can a man be pure before his Maker?" (Job 4:17). The trials Job went through weren't punishments, but they did test his faith. I believe Eliphaz unknowingly foreshadows the coming of Jesus Christ, who took the blame for all our sins so we can stand pure before God. Eliphaz reminds Job that we are mere mortals, "who dwell in houses of clay, whose foundation is in the dust, who are crushed like the moth" (Job 4:19). We cannot save ourselves, but Eliphaz is forgetting how much God loves His creation. God is just and must punish us for our sins, but He is also merciful and loving.

Through all of this, Job remains faithful to God. He never curses God, and he reminds his friends that our lives on earth are not eternal. He mentions that those who deny God spend their riches on earthly things that won't last. Job says, "Though he heap up silver like dust, and pile up clothing like clay, he may pile it up, but the righteous will wear it, and the innocent will divide the silver" (Job 27:16–17). Job is saying that you can have all the money in the world. You can be so rich that all of your finery is in such excess that it lays around as common as the dust or the clay of the ground. You have so many clothes, you can't wear them all, and your exorbitant wealth appears as ordinary dirt. Job says these things will not save you. Only faith in God can do that. Remember, this is the Old Testament, so Jesus had not come yet, but Job knew where his help came from: God.

The world makes it easy to forget God, especially when it comes to creativity and fame. The world loves to put artists on pedestals, saying they must be worshiped and copied for their gifts. We see this especially with fashion, music, and social media trends. Musicians who used to sell out stadiums are often forgotten by the next generation. Secondhand stores are full of clothes that were cool ten years ago. Hairstyles that once took hours to achieve are laughed at in old yearbooks. Remember to never worship the artist or seek worship from others for your art.

God has given us this ability to create and imagine. The truth is that it's God's creativity, which He chose to put inside of each of us. We did not earn creativity, nor did God forget or neglect to give creativity to some of us. We can hone our creative talents to improve them, but the fact that we each are creative comes solely as a gift from God. Going back to the very beginning of Job, he reminds us, "The LORD gave, and the LORD has taken away; blessed be the name of the LORD" (Job 1:21b). God gave us each the ability to be creative, and He has the power to remove the creative desires from our hearts when we use our skills for our own gain.

We read a similar passage in Acts. The author is instructing us not to think of God as a man-made idol, but to remember that He is real, and He is coming back. The author says there was a time when God overlooked our ignorance in worshiping man-made idols, but now God "commands all people everywhere to repent, because [He] has fixed a day on which [He] will judge the world in righteousness by a man whom [He] has appointed; and of this [He] has given assurance to all by raising [Him] from the dead" (Acts 17:30–31). This passage, I believe, is referencing the literal idols the people used to make and worship, and I also think this can refer to us today. What are the idols in our lives that we don't even realize are idols? Have we been worshiping our own creations more than we are praising God for giving us the ability to create?

As an artist, one thing I still struggle with is how to honor God with my creativity, and I highly doubt I'm the only one.

Yes, there are volunteer opportunities, but are these the only chances I get? Can I honor God with my art even if it does not have obvious Christian themes or is not volunteer work? Can I honor God through my work if I'm a hobby artist? What if I make art full time?

I believe we can honor God even if we are making money through selling our art and not just volunteering; it all just depends on how we go about it. Again, if our main goals involve trying to become famous, we need to watch out. We are told several times that fame and beauty are fleeting. The Lord's Kingdom is what lasts for eternity. Making sure we are honoring God through our art helps us stay focused on what matters. We must point all the glory back to the One who gave us the ability in the first place.

If you are making money through your creativity, good for you! Just make sure you are tithing as well. This counts as income, and the first fruits should go right back to God. This is another way we can honor Him and thank Him for all of His blessings He has bestowed upon us. We are also trusting in Him to provide for us because we are not being stingy with our income, hoarding it all for ourselves and our wants.

Third, going back to the beginning of this book, if we find joy in our creative process, then we are experiencing emotions that God intended for us. He allows us to be creative, not only to express ourselves but also to feel the joy that comes with creating. I can worship God by making pots because I see the symbolism now. If a piece is ruined on the wheel, I'm reminded of God's relationship with me. When I fire my pots, I think of the trials God has brought me through and will continue to bring me through. When I glaze the pieces, I consider God's grace. As long as our focus is on God and doing His will, we will honor Him. This is not to say that going to the studio replaces church for me. That is not the case at all, and every time I'm in the studio, I'm not singing hymns. We all need to be surrounded by fellow believers. Church is so important, which is why you will never find me working in my studio on a Sunday. What I mean by that statement is that we honor God by using the talents, creativity, and strengths He gave us to add enrichment into our own lives and reflect Him to those around us.

The benediction in Hebrews reminds us that God gives us the power and strength to do His will, not our own. Remember your Creator. Now that you know what might be an idol for you, it is time to remove it. The benediction says, "Now may the God of peace who brought again from the dead our Lord Jesus, the great shepherd of the sheep, by the blood of the eternal covenant, equip you with everything good that you may do his will, working in us that which is pleasing in his sight, through Jesus Christ, to whom be the glory forever and ever. Amen" (Hebrews 13:20–21). That is what I wish for you as you move forward, to remember that God is a peace-loving God. He has given you a certain skill set to do the tasks that only you can do. These tasks are things that will bring honor and glory to your father, the King of Heaven and Earth.

These words are meant to guide and encourage you. This book is designed to strengthen your faith and give you another angle from which to view your relationship with God. In no way have I set out to discourage you, but we all feel a little discouraged at times. Remember the devil wants you defeated and destroyed, but God has promised that He will continue to renew your spirit as long as you ask Him; remember Psalm 51:10 from Chapter 10 in this book. God will cleanse us and renew us.

God goes before us each day. He already knows what challenges we will face tomorrow and the five hundred tomorrows from now. Like giving the Israelites manna each morning, God will only provide us with the strength needed for each day. We must continually rely on Him. The more we cling to God, the more peace and joy we will find. Remember, "It is the LORD who goes before you. He will be with you; [He] will not leave you or forsake you. Do not fear or be dismayed" (Deuteronomy 31:8). God made us and has no desire to abandon us.

Right after the Israelites escaped from Egypt, once Pharaoh had demanded they leave, God guided His people on their journey. We see in Exodus, "The LORD went before them by day in a pillar

"God made us and has no desire to abandon us."

of cloud to lead them along the way, and by night in a pillar of fire to give them light, that they might travel by day and by night. The pillar of cloud by day and the pillar of fire by night did not depart from before the people" (Exodus 13:21–22). God came in the fire to guide His people out of captivity.

There is one other pottery technique you are probably familiar with, but I think it is worth mentioning. This technique has gained Western popularity relatively recently, but it is an ancient art form originating in Asia. To be more specific, it is the kintsugi technique from Japan. Kintsugi is an art form in and of itself, and it dates back hundreds of years. Essentially, when a ceramic (remember, *ceramic* refers to all types of clay) pot gets broken, a kintsugi artist will repair it using a type of adhesive and gold dust. The gold dust mixed with the glue highlights the cracked edges of the pot, making its flaws shine.

In today's fast-fashion culture, most of us don't just hang onto our broken coffee mugs. Kintsugi invites the viewer to consider the pot in a different way other than its functional usefulness. Just because the pot is broken, it doesn't mean it isn't valuable. Just because you feel unworthy, it doesn't make it true. The piece that is put back together by a kintsugi artist becomes more valuable than before.

How can that be right? It was broken; how can it be worth more now? That gold dust adds to the value of the piece and the overall time the artist takes with the piece also increases its worth. More importantly, the fact that the owner cares enough about the piece to go to the trouble to pay to have it fixed or to fix it herself shows this pot is valuable in the owner's eyes.

This is how God sees us. When earthly circumstances cause us to feel broken and irreparable, God sees us. When we can't get the words out in prayer through the waves of tears, God hears us. When we are so tired of struggling in this imperfect world and cry out to God in desperation, God knows us. When we are wide awake so filled with fear and worry that 1 a.m. feels more like 1 p.m., God is near. When we are hurting and feel like the pain will never go away, God comforts us. When we feel so embarrassed by a mistake we have made that it loops on repeat in our heads, God forgives us. All we have to do is ask Him and have faith that He will do what He says. Remember the Beatitudes:

"And he opened his mouth and taught them, saying: Blessed are the poor in spirit, for theirs is the kingdom of heaven, Blessed are those who mourn, for they shall be comforted. Blessed are the meek, for they shall inherit the earth. Blessed are those who hunger and thirst for righteousness, for they shall be satisfied. Blessed are the merciful, for they shall receive mercy. Blessed are the pure in heart, for they shall see God. Blessed are the peacemakers, for they shall be called sons of God. Blessed are those who are persecuted for righteousness' sake, for theirs is the kingdom of heaven. Blessed are you when others revile you and persecute you and utter all kinds of evil against you falsely on my account. Rejoice and be glad, for your reward is great in heaven" (Matthew 5:2-12).

God sees us in our brokenness and is gentle with us. He cares for His creation, remember?

Has something you made ever gotten broken? How did that cause you to feel? It can be devastating to see something you poured yourself into shatter on the ground. Sometimes we can repair it, like with kintsugi, but we are only human, so we can never make it new again.

God is willing and able to renew us whenever we ask it of Him. Every time we confess and ask forgiveness for our sins, He renews us. We appear as though we never sinned. Jesus paid for our mistakes with His life, so we are free. Like the pot needing time with the kintsugi artist, the more time we spend with God, the better we will feel and the more we will strive to be better. He tells us what is true, and through His truth, we can start to remove the lies of worthlessness that the world has been graffiti painting all over our minds. We didn't ask for these labels the world nails onto us. Jesus took the nails for us. Let Him set you free today.

 *Creativity Challenge:* We have come to our final creativity challenge. I hope that these have helped you to think outside the box and feel more comfortable being creative. For this last challenge, honor God through your creativity and don't stop creating!

Acknowledgments

So many people have aided me in this process and I thank God for the gifts that each one of you has been in my life. Thank you Mom and Dad for allowing me to study ceramics. Thank you, Mom, my prayer warrior, for putting me in that very first pottery class, for using your talents to proofread this book, and for always pointing me back to God. Thank you, Dad, for your sincere interest in my pottery endeavors, for encouraging me to go big, and for your late-night advice when we load the kiln together. Those are some of my favorite times. Thank you to my sister Leigh Marie for being the sister I need. You keep me laughing and humble, constantly providing the alternative angle to situations I seem to be stuck in. May the Lord guide you in your artistic journey.

Thank you to Tori Motyl, Delaney Harrigan, and Alyssa Ruberto for volunteering to proofread. I appreciate your selflessness in giving your time to read the rough copy. Each of you provided thoughtful insights that added little gems to this book. Thanks also to my fellow studio mates at Southside Studios in Asheville for always being ready and willing with perceptive feedback. Right when I needed you all, God provided.

Thank you to Morgan James Publishing for giving me this amazing opportunity. A special thanks to Terry Whalin, Naomi Chellis, and Addy Normann. Thank you all for never getting tired of answering my many, many questions. This book would have never made it to print without you. Thanks to my editor Cortney Donelson for handling the minutia. You are truly amazing at what you do. You came to my aid in the final hour and made this book quite beautiful.

Thank you to all of my pottery teachers, official and unofficial. You make the art world a better place by willingly sharing techniques and skills you could have easily kept to yourselves. Thank you for not laughing at my wonky beginner wheel-thrown pots and for showing me there's more to ceramics than just the wheel.

Thank you to all of the Christian influences in my life, especially Brookstone Church, my home church, in Weaverville, North Carolina. Thank you for always providing ways to grow closer to God. I have become a more knowledgeable and confident Christian under your roof. Thank you to my small group for your kind advice, encouragement, and listening ears.

To my fellow Christians walking in faith, never underestimate the power you have through the Holy Spirit inside you. I encourage you in Christ, as I have been encouraged.

What's Next

See what Morgan is up to at her website www.morgan-mccarver.com. There you will find upcoming festivals and exhibitions. You will also be able to message her, sign up for the newsletter, and shop for her pottery online. Stay connected on Instagram: @morgan_mccarver_porcelain , Facebook: @Morgan McCarver, Twitter: @GodTheArtistBk

If you are interested in getting covered in clay, local ceramics centers and potters in the area are great places to start when looking for classes.

If you are interested in getting covered in the love of Jesus, local churches are a great place to start!

Feel free to ask Morgan any questions that you might have about pottery and Christianity. If she is unable to answer, she will connect you with someone who can! She is looking forward to seeing some pictures of completed creativity challenges as well!

About the Author

Morgan **McCarver** is a multi-award-winning ceramic artist based in Asheville, North Carolina. After a scoliosis spinal fusion surgery made it impossible for her to dance during recovery, she redirected her creative energy and discovered a passion for clay while taking a summer pottery class. This inspired her to pursue a degree in ceramics from Anderson University in South Carolina, where she had the honor of receiving the 2019 Outstanding Art Major Ceramics Award.

She established her own business, Morgan McCarver Porcelain in 2019 and has studios in Asheville, North Carolina, and Spartanburg, South Carolina. Her work has been featured in galleries and juried exhibitions across the United States. Some of the highlights include being a 2020 701 Center for Contemporary Art prize finalist, where she had the honor of being the youngest artist to ever make it that far. She has displayed her work in two solo exhibitions, "FemininiTEA" 2020 and "The Strength of a Wildflower" 2022. She also completed residencies at Edgewood Cottage in Blowing Rock, 2022 and 2023. She became a recipient of the North Carolina Arts Council Artist Support Grant, allowing her to attend the National Council on Education for the Ceramic Arts for the first time. She has several copyrights on her floral drawings that she screen-prints onto her porcelain. Her art can be found in various galleries around the Carolinas and Tennessee, as well as on her website, www.morganmccarver. com, and her Etsy shop, MorganMPorcelain. She spends most of her days in her studio, crafting beautiful works of art, while Sundays are reserved for church. As an active member of Brookstone Church in Weaverville, North Carolina, she enjoys spending time with her small group and volunteering as a youth leader.

Endnotes

Chapter 1

Exodus 31:1–5
Exodus 35:34–35
Exodus 26:2–3
Merriam-Webster Dictionary, s.v. "Create (*verb*)," accessed
    June 12, 2023, https://www.merriam-webster.com/
    dictionary/create.

Chapter 2

Genesis 1:1–2
Isaiah 43:1
Psalm 135:6

Genesis 1:26

Genesis 1:27

Genesis 2:7

Isaiah 40:8

Matthew 6:28–30

Genesis 1:31

Genesis 2:19

Bayles, David and Ted Orland, *Art and Fear: Observations On The Perils (and Rewards) of ARTMAKING* (Santa Cruz, CA: Image Continuum Press, 2001), 14–16.

Chapter 3

John 10:10

Psalm 150:6

Psalm 23

Ephesians 2:10

Luke 19:40

Colossians 3:23–24

Regarding Yahweh: https://www.gotquestions.org/breathe-Yahweh.html

Chapter 4

Jeremiah 10:12–13

Romans 1:20

Psalm 104:24

Psalm 139:15

Job 10:9

Ecclesiastes 1:9

Romans 11:36

Chapter 5

Brett Smith, "How are Technical Ceramics used in Space Programs?" *AZoM*, (March 2021): accessed June 12, 2023, https://www.azom.com/article.aspx?ArticleID=20203.

"Ceramic Hip Replacements," The Center for Reconstructive Surgery, (November 2021): accessed June 12, 2023, https://drharwin.com/joint-replacement/ceramic-hip-replacements/.

Genesis 3:19
Romans 12:4–8
2 Corinthians 5:17
1 Corinthians 12:4–11

Chapter 6

Wood, Bryant G. PhD. "THE MASTER POTTER: POTTERY MAKING IN THE BIBLE." Biblioarcheology.Org/Research. Associates for Biblical Research, July 5, 2011.

Isaiah 41:25
Mark 15:34
Isaiah 55:6–8
Psalm 22:1
Revelation 1:4–5
Psalm 18:2
Daniel 2:41–44

Chapter 7

Isaiah 66:2
Luke 1:37
Romans 12:2

1 Corinthians 3:10–11
John 17:14–15

Chapter 8
Proverbs 4:27
Matthew 7:14
2 Timothy 2:19
Matthew 14:30–31
Isaiah 64:8
John 1:3
Ezekiel 5:5–6

Chapter 9
2 Corinthians 2:14
Ecclesiastes 11:10
Isaiah 1:16–17
Jeremiah 4:1–2
Luke 15:21–24
Luke 15:28–30
Luke 15:31–32
Matthew 18:9
Isaiah 45:9
Isaiah 29:16

Chapter 10
Psalm 22:14–15
John 4:10
Exodus 8:19
Exodus 12:30–32

Proverbs 28:14

John 7:38

2 Corinthians 5:17

Deuteronomy 29:18–20

Psalm 51:10

Psalm 63:1

Isaiah 44:3

James 4:8

Crosta, Peter. "What You Should Know about Dehydration." Medical News Today. December 20, 2017, accessed June 12, 2023, https://www.medicalnewstoday.com/ articles/153363.

Chapter 11

1 Corinthians 3:12–15

Daniel 3:25

Jonah 2:1–10

Exodus 9:8–10

James 1:2

1 Peter 1:6–8

2 Peter 2:9

Deuteronomy 31:8

Galatians 6:2

"What Is the Gold Melting Point?" Gold Rush Trading Post. Accessed June 12, 2023. https://www.goldrushtradingpost. com/gold_melting_point.

Chapter 12

Romans 9:19–21

2 Timothy 2:20–21
Esther 4:13–14
Matthew 6:26–30
Proverbs 26:23
2 Samuel 17:27–29
Lamentations 4:2
Revelation 2:26–28

Chapter 13
1 Peter 5:8
Exodus 19:18
Matthew 25:46
1 Chronicles 4:23
Matthew 25:31–32
Leviticus 20:25–26
Ezra 10:10–11
Nehemiah 9:2
Numbers 16:21
Isaiah 30:14
2 Corinthians 4:7
Psalm 2:9
Grenson, Jessica. "19 Different Types of Kilns for Pottery (Complete List)." TypesofKilns.com. Accessed June 12, 2023. https://typesofkilns.com/.

Chapter 14
Job 13:12
Nahum 3:14
1 Kings 7:45–46

2 Chronicles 4:17

Matthew 27:7–10

Zechariah 11:12–14

John 10:11

Jeremiah 18:3–6

Romans 8:28

Jeremiah 19:1–3

Revelation 21:18–22

Bahde, Thomas. "THE COMMON DUST OF POTTER'S FIELD." *Commonplace: The Journal of Early American Life,* volume 6, no. 4 (2006). Accessed June 12, 2023. http://commonplace.online/article/the-common-dust-of-potters-field/#:~:text=It%20originated%20in%20Matthew%2027,for%20the%20burial%20of%20strangers.

Chapter 15

Job 4:17–19

Job 27:16–17

Job 1:21

Acts 17:29–31

Hebrews 13:20–21

Deuteronomy 31:8

Exodus 13:21–22

Matthew 5:2–12

A free ebook edition is available with the purchase of this book.

To claim your free ebook edition:

1. Visit MorganJamesBOGO.com
2. Sign your name CLEARLY in the space
3. Complete the form and submit a photo of the entire copyright page
4. You or your friend can download the ebook to your preferred device

Print & Digital Together Forever.

Snap a photo

Free ebook

Read anywhere

Printed in the USA
CPSIA information can be obtained
at www.ICGtesting.com
JSHW020745201223
53967JS00002B/22

9 781636 982038